5 +/24 $2

NO BURDEN TO CARRY

NO BURDEN TO CARRY

Narratives of Black Working Women
in Ontario 1920s – 1950s

Dionne Brand

with the assistance of Lois De Shield
and the Immigrant Women's Job Placement Centre

women's
P R E S S

CANADIAN CATALOGUING IN PUBLICATION DATA
Brand, Dionne, 1953 –
No Burden to Carry: Narratives of Black Working Women in
Ontario 1920s–1950s

ISBN 0-88961-163-7

1. Women, Black – Ontario – History. 2. Women, Black – Employment – Ontario
– History. 3. Sex discrimination in employment – Ontario – History. 4. Racism –
Ontario – History. I. Title.

FC3100.B6B7 1991   971.3'00496   C91-095100-4   F1059.7.N3B7 1991

Editing: P.K. Murphy
Copy editing: Nuzhat Amin
Cover design: Grace Channer with the assistance of Sunday Harrison
Cover photograph from GICO Ammunitions Plant Newsletter

For information address Women's Press, Suite 233, 517 College Street, Toronto,
Ontario, Canada M6G 4A2

This book was produced by the collective effort of Women's Press.
Women's Press gratefully acknowledges financial support from the Canada
Council and the Ontario Arts Council.

Printed and bound in Canada.
1 2 3 4 5   1995 1994 1993 1992 1991

This book is dedicated to Lois De Shield.

Contents

Acknowledgements

The oral history research was sponsored by The Immigrant Women's Job Placement Centre. Lois De Shield and Leila Imeish of the Centre gave all of their time and support to the project. Fifty women in all were interviewed and many women worked on this project. I would like to extend my deep gratitude to my co-interviewers, Lois De Shield, Adrienne Shadd, Patricia Hayes, Carol Allain, Linda Carty and Ayanna Black. They used their own resources, links and sense of Black life in order to pull the project together. Faith Nolan's insistence that Black Canadian history never be forgotten and the use of her collection of books on Black Canadian history led me in great part to this work. For this I thank her. Also Barb Taylor; her long and painstaking hours of transcription were absolutely invaluable. My gratitude to Pat Murphy for a two-year collaboration on editing these narratives. Other people I wish to thank are Krisantha Sri Bhaggiyadatta, Dionne Falconer and Peggy Bristow. I also wish to thank the Ministry of Culture (Heritage Branch) and the Ontario Women's Directorate for their funding. All royalties from this book go to the Immigrant Women's Job Placement Centre.

Interviewers
Dionne Brand, Lois De Shield, Adrienne Shadd, Patricia Hayes, Carol Allain, Linda Carty, Ayanna Black

No Burden to Carry

i

The history of Black people in Canada, let alone the history of Black women in Canada, has not been taken up by many Canadian scholars. Where information exists on Black history, it is usually general. Analyses, though well-intended, have been sweeping in their approach, as if a single work could uncover the complexity of the existence of any people, or have taken the point of view of Canada as simply a haven from United States slavery. When they have tried to be definitive, they have only been cursory; when substantive, they have preoccupied themselves with integration as the goal of Black people. Those who have tried to recover the continuities and linkages have sacrificed detail and have, therefore, been unable to insert more than an outline of an existing people within "the Canadian milieu." Canadian scholarship overall has been preoccupied with English and French concerns, to the exclusion of Canadian peoples of non-European origin. This, at best, is xenophobic; it is also racist. Black life is treated as static and finite, against which "Canadian" life, read "white," is

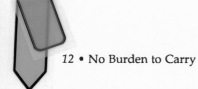

ongoing and changing, the recording of the latter taking precedence and importance, the former footnoted.

Inquiry into the history of Blacks in Canada has, on the whole, assumed that it is possible to know all there is to know about the subject at a glance. If Black life in Canada as a whole has been absent from the works of Canadian scholars, or inadequately served by them, Black women's lives have been doubly hidden. Within existing accounts, Black peoples are taken as a genderless group. The occasional woman in history is highlighted, such as Mary Ann Shadd, the nineteenth-century teacher, publisher and editor, or Harriet Tubman, the freedom fighter, abolitionist and general of the Underground Railroad. But these high-lights are exceptions, and their heroic behaviour is attributed to their race rather than to their gender, despite the fact that they were extraordinary women who broke the norms of female behaviour of the day. Of course, they were *Black* women, for whom female existence differed greatly from that of white women.

Taking Black peoples in Canada as a genderless group conflates all of Black history into the history of men doing things. Yet one might even go further and say that because the ideology of masculinity also differed and differs for Black men and white men, Black history is both de-feminised as well as, to a lesser extent, de-masculinised, but the outcome nevertheless subordinates the experiences of Black women in Canadian history to those of Black men. The sexual division of labour is subsumed in the racial division of labour, and "the race" is conflated into and narrowed to its male members.

Nor has feminist scholarship picked up on the lives of Black women except in cursory ways, or in what has come to be known as the "added on" theory — the off-hand addition of information on Black women after their absence has been pointed out.

The excavation of Black women's history in Canada by Black women scholars is in its formative stages, and we can hope and look forward to the "discovery" of Black women's lives in Canada from their first arrival some 270 years ago to the present.

In trying to recover this history, I take the position that a "historical fact" is somewhat more flexible or self-interested than we are normally led to believe, that history has tended to be written by men and about men.[1] Moreover, I take the position that Black history has tended to excise the place of Black women in it and that to recover Black women as historical actors is not only to clarify the historical record but ultimately to recover a revolutionary method for feminist struggle and Black struggle.

Joan Kelly writes that feminist historiography "has disabused us of the notion that the history of women is the same as the history of men, and that significant turning points in history have the same impact for one sex as for the other."[2] Indeed, by virtue of gender, the history of Black women is not the *same* as the history of Black men, and if we were to return to that most significant point in history for Black people in the Americas, slavery, we would find that the underpinnings of sexism and patriarchy structured that institution as to exploit women and men in different ways. With Black history this point was until recently more often than not blurred, obfuscated not only because men wrote history but because in our case race dominates and writes history and race writes gender outside and beyond history.[3]

This book of narratives of Black working women looks at some of the particularities of Black women's lives in

Ontario from the 1920s to the 1950s, so that we may look at them in their complexity.

ii

The abolition of slavery, that whole institution which gave rise to the presence of their great-grandmothers and -grandfathers on Canadian soil, was not one hundred years old when the women in these narratives were born. And the abolition of slavery did not eradicate racism as an organising principle within the social, economic or political life of Canada and the United States. Their mothers and grandmothers before them worked in fields, tended chickens and hogs, washed, ironed, cooked and cleaned for a wage and took care of children, grandchildren and family. In the small farming communities of Ontario, and in cities like Toronto and Windsor, they and their husbands made do within the racially stratified society which positioned them in precarious proximity to a living wage. Getting by was equally difficult for rural and urban women, even though some rural families owned their own farms. Accounts here show more than a passing similarity of experience between rural and urban women as the Depression saw many farm daughters move to the cities to seek work in the 1920s and 1930s. This migration to the cities suggests the difficulties of farm life in that period and the impact of the Depression in rural areas.

In her essay "Domestic Service in Canada 1880–1920," Genevieve Leslie argues that domestic service changed with industrialisation. "The period 1880–1920 ... was a transitional period which clearly revealed the incompatibility of domestic service and modern industrial trends ... in 1891 domestics accounted for 41 percent of the female work force, and were by far the largest single group of workers; by 1921 domestics represented only 18 percent of all employed women but were still the second largest category of female workers."[4] Since their arrival in Ontario, first as slaves then as fugitives from slavery in the early 1800s, Black women had worked on farms, in domestic service and at home. Indications are that not until 1940 or so did any significant number of them work at industrial labour. Certainly up to the Second World War at least 80 percent of Black women in Canadian cities worked in domestic service.[5] Industrialisation did not have the overwhelming impact on Black women wage earners that it did on white women. The situation of Black women working as domestics seems to have been similar in the United States. Jacqueline Jones, in her exhaustive treatment of Black women and work in the United States, points out, "In 1940 one third of all white, but only 1.3 percent of all black working women had clerical jobs. On the other hand, 60 percent of all black female workers were domestic servants; the figure for white women was only 10 percent."[6]

The effects of the Depression that began in 1929 were, of course, severe for the Black population in Canada. Already marginalised in the economy because of their colour, and in the case of women because of both their colour and their gender, the scarcity of work and wage made them reach even deeper for ways of stretching their limited resources. But so used to hardship was the community that when asked how the Depression was for Black people, one woman in these narratives remarked that the community was closer-knit than the white community, so they shared whatever they had. She added that Black people didn't "suffer as much" because "we were used to doing without."

Those Black rural women in Ontario during the Depression who remained on the farms barely made a living raising chickens and cultivating gardens for the family food. Some families moved from small town to small town, the men doing general labour and the women taking care of the children and, where possible, growing food. Other families, urban and rural, survived on the wages of husbands and sons working as porters on the railroad. (Working as a porter on the railroad was to Black men what domestic work was to Black women.)

Yet these were also the decades of the Garvey movement and union organising — the Universal Negro Improvement Association (UNIA) and the Order of Sleeping Car Porters and the Brotherhood of Sleeping Car Porters. Black Canadian women played important roles within these movements.

Garveyism was perhaps the first secular movement to rival the magnetism of the church in the Black community in Canada. This philosophy, organised through the Universal Negro Improvement Association and under the leadership of Marcus Mosiah Garvey, advocated self-government and self-determination for Black peoples in the Americas. It advocated race pride, building a Black nation through the acquisition of capital, as well as repatriation to and reclamation of Africa (Liberia in particular) as the true homeland. The movement itself began in 1914, in Jamaica where Garvey was born, and spread throughout the United States, Canada and Britain. In Toronto and Montreal chapters of the UNIA were established in 1919. Garvey fired the imagination of many Black Torontonians in the 1920s and 1930s, pointing to how Black people could actively organise against the racist social and economic conditions. The movement was not merely ideological; nor was its rhetoric without practical application. Properties were bought out of dues and pledges, and Garvey began the Black Star Lines, a shipping company incorporated to trade in rubber from Liberia.[7] Black Torontonians plunged into organising — the women no less vigorously than the men. Several women in the narratives recall the movement; one, Violet Blackman who died in 1990, was a true stalwart of the UNIA in Toronto from its outset. Her account suggests that many other women also engaged in domestic service worked in the cause of the UNIA.

The long and arduous union organising of the Brotherhood of Sleeping Car Porters against racism on the CNR and CPR (Black men were excluded from joining white railway unions) and for their right to collective bargaining made the period 1918–1945 one which galvanised the Black community in Canada to its own defence.[8] Black women, the wives of porters, became active in the auxiliaries of the Brotherhood, extending the new politicisation into community organising and education. They organised Negro History weeks and raised money for educational scholarships well into the late 1950s.

Of the early Black church in Canada Robin Winks remarks peculiarly, "While these churches usually were fragments of Protestantism, they frequently cut themselves off from the larger body, and tended to be theologically stagnant. Many reinforced the stereotype so beloved by white Christians — that of the noble black ready to bear suffering for the Lord because, in the end, the Lord has the whole wide world in his hands — for the Negro churches often lacked intellectual conviction while possessing an abundance of emotion and faith."[9] Given the racial segregation of the period (well-documented by Winks himself), one wonders at Winks' conclusion that Black churches "cut themselves off." Doubtless the churches were conservative in their thinking as to a way forward for Blacks, but that seems more a feature of Christianity, and "cutting themselves off" seems more a tactic for survival and self-preservation than the failure that Winks suggests.

Through the church, however, as Winks later observes astutely, "black men blazed their own segregated paths toward high office."[10] Black women, needless to say, were excluded from positions of real power, namely ordination as ministers, until the ordination of Addie Aylestock in 1951 in the British Methodist Episcopal Church — more than 100 years after its founding in 1856. Though women were not found in positions of power in the Black church, they were certainly to be found in traditional positions of responsibility. The missionary societies of the churches were the organisations which harnessed the aspirations as well as the woman power which drove the very engine of the churches. Missionary work was women's work. The women of the missionary societies visited the sick, raised money for those in need here and in Africa and organised the social life of the Black community. Black women's organising through missionary societies spans more than a century in Canada. They emerged in 1882, with the establishment of the Women's Home Missionary Society in the Baptist faith. Mary Branton, a Baptist missionary born in Chatham in 1860, founded a school in South Africa and did missionary work in Liberia.[11]

Winks does not mention Addie Aylestock's ordination in the British Methodist Episcopal Church in 1951. Chiefly concerned in his analysis with "how the Negro and white come to terms with each other," Winks' work also hangs on Black upliftment (not always in the best sense of the word). Like other Canadian historians on the subject, he does not consider the lot of Black women as at times different from that of Black men. Nor do Winks and others consider Black women worthy of even a minor focus. It is quite possible, indeed probable, that Black women themselves did not see their condition as different from that of Black men; rather, in the *de facto* and sometimes *de jure* race segregation which existed in Canada they would have measured their condition against the condition of white women and not against that of Black men. The patriarchal structures which underlie political, economic and social life were not the subject of their daily preoccupations and were rarely the subject of internal quarrels in the Black community, at least never to the extent of occasioning a schism. But the structures existed, and once in a while the conflicts were manifested in women's outspokenness. Mary Ann Shadd in an 1855 editorial in her newspaper *Provincial Freeman* wrote sarcastically to Black male critics of her role as a community spokeswoman, "… it is fit that you should deport your ugliest to a woman. To coloured women, we have 'broken the Editorial Ice' for your class in America; so go to Editing, as many of you as are willing and able."[12] More benign was the formation of benevolent societies, mothers' leagues for the teaching of household duties to Negro girls and also women's clubs, such as the Negro Women's Club, formed in Montreal in 1902, and the Eureka Club, formed in 1910 in Toronto. Black upliftment and welfare might have been a more central concern than women's emancipation to these groups, but they cannot be examined solely within that context for they also signified the gender uplift of Black women. The institution of slavery had so degraded Black womanhood that the establishment of women's clubs and ladies' auxiliaries must be seen within the context of the rehabilitation of the images of Black womanhood and as fortresses against the invasions of white domination over Black female sexuality.

iii

Ruth Roach Pierson, in her book on Canadian women in World War II states, "Canada's War effort, rather than any consideration of women's right to work, determined the recruitment of women into the labour force. The recruitment of women was part of a large-scale intervention by Government into the labour market to control allocation of labour for effective prosecution of war."[13] This was no less true for the women in these narratives. Nor was racial desegregation an objective of the war effort. Ghettoised up to then in domestic work of one sort or another — mothers' helpers, housekeeping, laundry work, general help, etc. — the war effort released Black women from the racialised, segregated, female employment that for them was domestic work and marked their entry into industrial labour and clerical work. "Things opened up," many women say. They also opened up for Black men who were recruited into the armed forces.

Though the Canadian Army at first rejected Black volunteers, Winks reports that by 1941 it had dropped its most blatant racial policies, though the nature of service allowed Black servicemen still reflected the racism of the society.[14] In her narrative one woman recounts trying, as she says, "to sell my colour to the army," but giving up after getting what she calls the "runaround." Winks suggests that racism decreased during World War II, stating "Thus the total impact of World War II was an educational one for white and black, bettering the status of the Negro worker — in and out of uniform — throughout Canada and The North."[15] But racism did not so much decrease as that mobilisation for the war effort made it expedient to do away with some of the more primitive racial restrictions in order to free all the productive forces in the service of winning the war. According to Winks, until 1942 the National Selective Service accepted racial restrictions from employers. In 1942, according to Pierson, the NSS (Women's Division) began a drive to register and recruit much-needed female labour for the war industry and essential services.

As many in these narratives attest, Black women would not have needed much encouragement to flee race-bound domestic work. Most here were well within the age group most favoured for recruitment, single and 20-24 years old. Though some were married, by mid-1943 the National Selective Service were recruiting them too.[16] Indeed, given the extent of the labour shortages, there was a lot of room for Black women. "By mid 1943 there were labour shortages in service jobs long dependent on female (*i.e.*, *white*) labour. Women were leaving these for higher paying employment in war industries. Hospitals, restaurants, hotels, laundries, and dry cleaners were clamouring for help, but the labour pool of single women available for full time employment was exhausted."[17] Then too, as Pierson points out, even non-essential jobs like candy, tobacco and soft drink companies[18] were experiencing labour shortages.

Widespread expansion of goods and services which the war occasioned made possible and palatable the employment of Black women in jobs where their employment was once unacceptable both in terms of their race and their sex. But the nation-wide publicity campaigns undertaken by the NSS to persuade women to sign up for work were neither directed toward Black women nor were their slogans of patriotism instrumental in recruiting Black women. Simply put, Black women needed the work, they needed the money, and waged work had been an essential part of their daily lives. James Walker points out, "In 1941, 80 percent of Black adult females in Montreal were employed as domestic servants."[19] By all accounts, this was also the case in Toronto, Windsor and London. And as domestic workers, usually beginning their working lives at fifteen, Black women's wages ranged from fifteen to thirty dollars a month in conditions of employment which could subject them to such arbitrary demands as foregoing time off, sixteen-hour days, and clothing in lieu of wages. Racism created an atmosphere where Black women's presence was on sufferance. So the industrial wage, the wholesale war recruitment that suggested that one's chances were as good as anyone else's, the anonymity of industrial labourers, and the indications of Black progress that this opportunity signalled were all a boon to Black women and to the Black community as a whole, despite the laissez faire racism on the job in the war plants and other industries.

There is some evidence that suggests the kind of treatment Black women as a whole experienced in the munitions plants. One woman refers to working on the "high explosives" side in one munitions plant. Another remarks that she felt that another Black woman was given a certain dangerous position on the line, making grenades, because of her race.

A few of the narratives suggest that some Black women felt freer at least to argue against racism on equal footing with the white women they encountered at their war jobs. The narrative of one woman on war work also suggests that she encountered for the first time the unusual circumstance of "... more Blacks (than) in any other jobs that I worked on." Another left teaching in the Maritimes for the service in Ottawa, having been recruited through the Selective Service. Still another became a teacher, recruited through a government war programme which offered grades twelve and thirteen students $45 to train as teachers, and another cites the fact that men teachers had been recruited into the armed forces, precipitating the recruitment of women as teachers. Though teaching was the other traditional job for a Black woman (there being segregated one-room schoolhouses in Black communities in the Maritimes and Ontario), World War II obviously opened up the number of jobs available in the profession.[20]

According to Pierson, "In addition to the wartime recruitment of women into industries and services, there was also recruitment of women into agriculture to 'fill some of the gaps in farm manpower with female labour.'" In all provinces farmers' wives and daughters took over farm work in the absence of male relatives and farm workers who had left the land to join the armed forces or to work in industry.[21]

Some women, particularly those from southwestern Ontario, might have been part of the Women's Land Brigade and Farm Girls Brigades of the Farm Labour Service, as some recount working not only in their own fields but also hiring out as farm help. Working their own fields, however, or hiring out as farm help would not have been unusual for these women under ordinary circumstances, since some of them had husbands, brothers and fathers who worked on the railroads as porters and the women were already carrying the load of farm work. Others already worked planting tobacco or picking tomatoes and cucumbers.

As Pierson[22] has found, despite the recruitment campaigns which stressed patriotic duty, the real motivation of women entering the wartime job market was indeed not for the most part because of the need to do patriotic service but from economic necessity. This was perhaps even more true for Black women workers of the time. Black women did see these jobs as a gain for the race, but much to their chagrin, no sooner had they fled domestic work than the retrenchment of women workers at the end of the war began, supposedly back "into traditionally female occupations."[23] In their case, however, retrenchment was also accompanied by an infusion of Black Caribbean women recruited by the department of immigration for domestic work in Canada.

While no Canadian historian has traced the course, consequences and significance of Black women's war work in Canada, Jacqueline Jones, in her formidable historical study of Black women and work in the United States, writes of the period, "From official United States Government posters to short stories in popular women's magazines, recruitment propaganda was aimed exclusively at white women of both the middle and working classes. When Black women were mentioned in connection with the national manpower crisis at all, they were exhorted to enter 'war services' by taking jobs that white women most readily abandoned — laundry, cafeteria, and domestic work.... While male workers might absent themselves from the factory as a result of overindulgence the night before, (white) female workers stayed home periodically to catch up on their washing, cleaning, and grocery shopping. Black women thus were supposed to form a behind-the-scenes cadre of support workers for gainfully employed white wives."[24]

Though the proportion of Black women was smaller in Canada, the same racial and sexual division of labour determined their entry and location in war work. Black women in the United States had a longer history of factory work than Black women in Canada. While Black women in the United States had what Jones describes as a "weak hold on industrial position" from the 1920s to the 1940s (seven percent of Black women in 1920, five and a half percent in 1930, six percent in 1940[25]), Black women in Canada seemed to have had no hold at all. Repeatedly in these narratives, the women say that Black women could not get any position but that of domestic work before the war.

Their foothold in factory work in the 1940s was, therefore, even more precarious than that of their sisters to the south. Isolated, and in smaller numbers in Toronto, Windsor, Chatham, and small communities in Ontario, the chances of collective action were much more slim. The experiences on the war time shop floor, however, inspired a militancy that would carry two of the women in these narratives on to union organising in Barrie and Chatham. The similarities between their experience in war work in Canada and the wartime experiences of Black women in the United States are worth noting in Canada which sees itself — unlike the United States — as not having a legacy of racism at the core of its social, political and economic development. Of the experience of Black women in the United States during the war Jones writes, "Often black women found their hard-won jobs in industry were not only segregated but the most dangerous and gruelling ones that a factory had to offer. During the war, certain men's jobs were converted to women's work and in the process downgraded to lower pay and status, but others were converted to Black women's work of even greater inferiority. In aeroplane assembly plants, Black women stood in stifling 'dope rooms' filled with the nauseating fumes of glue, while white women sat on stools in the well ventilated serving room ... elsewhere Black women worked in ammunitions and gunpowder, poisonous plastic and acetone, scaling mud and hazardous equipment ... Furthermore, they were routinely assigned 'discouraging' night shifts that imposed additional burdens on them as wives and mothers."[26]

Albeit dressed up in patriotism, war factory work in the 1940s could not have been a bed of roses for white women either, but racism could be counted on to structure the shop floor and to exact the most harsh penalties from Black women. To show that every step of the way to equality was going to be a fight and that mere entry into industrial labour could not eradicate racism, in 1946 Viola Desmond, a Black woman in New Glasgow, Nova Scotia, was arrested. She spent a night in jail, went to trial and was fined, all for sitting in the white section of a movie theatre. But as an old Black saying goes, 'You cut your dress to suit your cloth,' so despite the endemic racism in work and social structures, Black women in Canada latched on to the industrial wage and hung on for dear life.

They did not wish to return to the white people's kitchens where there was isolation, no fair wage, no chance of mobility, nor any recourse against the "personalised" racism of the employer. In a look at what she calls "Black Women Workers Demobilised and Redomesticated," Jacqueline Jones examines the impact of the end of the war on Black women workers: "A government researcher noted that reconversion affected Negroes more severely than white workers: from July 1945 to April 1946, for example, unemployment rates among non-whites increased more than twice as much as among whites... By 1948 most of the gains that Blacks had derived from the wartime boom had been wiped out, and labour analysts predicted that, given the persistent marginality of black workers, their well-being depended almost entirely on a strong economy."[27]

Many Black women now tried to escape domestic work. Most of the women in these narratives did escape, but they faced hard times combining part-time work, child rearing and efforts to seek work and careers outside of domestic work. But if they were reluctant to go back to domestic work, their Black Caribbean sisters were not. Fleeing the bust of Caribbean economies in the 1950s, Black women from the Caribbean came to Canada to fill the shortages in domestic workers.

Martin and Segrave examine the state of domestic work in Canada after the war. "At the end of the war the Canadian housewife faced the same domestic crisis (as in the U.S.). For Canada the solution lay in immigration, with thousands to be admitted into the country to become domestics. This practice was aided and abetted by the Canadian Government which did the recruiting in Europe. The Senate Committee on Immigration and Labour, in an August 1946 report, specifically mentioned the desirability of letting experienced foreign servants into the country."[28] What Martin and Segrave overlook is that when by 1949 the importation of European servants failed to make up the shortage, Black Caribbean women were imported to do the job. Nowhere do Martin and Segrave mention race as a factor in the Canadian "servant problem." They do not mention the Caribbean Domestic Worker Scheme of the 1950s (some threatened with deportation in the 1970s), nor do they mention the undoubtedly dubious but neverthe-less racial distinction between European women imported as "nannies" and Caribbean women as "domestics." While European women imported for domestic work would later blend into the white face of Canada, Black Caribbean women brought in to work as domestic workers would reinforce the stereotype of the Black woman as servant. Well into the 1960s and beyond Black women continued to fight for a foothold in non-domestic labour. Even today a disproportionate number of Black women work in institutionalised domestic work, as nursing attendants and health care aids and in other service sector jobs.

iv
"Oh jazz, dear!"

When I began doing the oral histories of Black women in Ontario I had read Nell Painter's *The Narrative of Hosea Hudson: His Life as a Negro Communist in the South* (1979), Dorothy Sterling's *We are Your Sisters* (1984), Jacqueline Jones' *Labour of Love, Labour of Sorrow* (1985), Paula Giddings' *When and Where I Enter* (1984), Gerder Lerner's *Black Women in White America* (1973), and a number of other Black or working-class histories. I was inspired by their attention to Black women's lives and, in the case of Nell Painter, to the detailing of working-class African-American male life. Hosea Hudson's beautiful recounting of the 1930s to the 1950s, and his evolution from sharecropper to political activist, is one of the most moving accounts of Black life I have read. These authors were writing about my history and the history that I shared with so many other people. I had read them because they had written about Black women or Black people and because all my life, from colonial dame school to post-graduate work in North

America, from "see Dick run" to Habermas, I had been forced to read and learn about white people.

Any Black works that I had read, even male-centred Black work, had not been taught in any white academic setting, but I had found these works firstly in the academy of the Black Power movement and socialist thought and later in the university of activism, feminism and Black feminist thought.

Of course, even outside the white academy, patriarchy was written into the texts which were themselves written to oppose race-biased texts. At any rate, I concentrated on reading whatever material existed that addressed the issues of Blacks, and when writing began to emerge about Black women I was even more enthusiastic. My recognition that work produced on Black peoples did not in the main include Black women led me to feminist inquiry. Discomfort over the fact that something was missing in Black history overcame me. Like most Black feminists, it also overcame me in feminist theory. Something was also missing there.

Gayatri Spivak, in her essay, "Three Women's Texts and a Critique of Imperialism," observes what is missing, in her critique of the nineteenth-century Brontë novel *Jane Eyre*. Even as Jane Eyre becomes the nineteenth century "feminist individualist," the novel is set against the mad woman in the attic (a white creole from Jamaica), a figure "produced by the axiomatics of imperialism."[29] Spivak persuasively presents the argument that, "It is the active ideology of imperialism that provides the discursive field" for Jane Eyre. Further, while Spivak credits Jean Rhys in *Wide Sargasso Sea* with the reinscribing or rewriting of Bertha Mason (Antoinette), the woman in the attic, as human rather than as the uncivilised object of the ideology of "imperialism as social mission,"[30] the critic points out that upon Rhys' reinscription of Bertha (Antoinette), another figure, Christophine, Antoinette's Black nurse, is built tangentially, is half missing.

These missing elements led me to work on the precise social construction of Black women's lives, the ways in which we live every day, our place in the political, economic and social structures and to an undertaking in oral history. My method developed out of a certainty that there must be something else to tell, something I had not yet heard articulated about Black women's lives in Canada. If we were to ask Black women themselves how they lived, what they thought about this or that, what would they say? My purpose is to unchain these histories from the genderless bundle of information and misinformation on "Blacks," both by outside groups (whites) and inside groups (Blacks).

Collecting that history, of course, presents numerous problems. What passes for the historical record in this country, feminist or mainstream, is simply faulty. The status of Black peoples in Canadian society, the existence of racism as an organising principle here in the past and in the present militated and militates against the existence of such records. As part of a rather small group investigating Black women's history in Canada, I decided to use the method of oral history to bring into high relief the terrain of Black women's lives.

In 1988 I initiated an oral history project, *The Lives of Black Working Women in Ontario,* under the sponsorship of The Immigrant Women's Job Placement Centre. In all, there were five other interviewers on the project. This project interviewed approximately fifty women, half of whom were over sixty years of age. Later the older women became the focus of the project for several reasons, primarily the necessity to take their histories in light of the advance of time and the possible failure of memory. Also, these women could talk about Black women's lives in the 1920s, 1930s, 1940s and 1950s, decades which seem to be missing in the historical record of Black life in Canada. Was the Depression, as one woman said, "not so bad for Black people because we knew how to do without"? Most of the women in this age category turned out to be Canadian-born, their people having come to Canada in the 1830s– 1860s.

The dearth of information about and references to Black women's history led me to employ oral history as a method of inquiry. But this was not the only reason: the historical relationship between Black peoples in Canada and "mainstream" society has been one of subordination, which doubtlessly taints a historical record often written by, spoken about and interpreted by those who hold power within the relationship. An oral history, therefore, affords a primacy to the opinions and interpretations of the people so subjected. Of course, it is also necessary to pose these hidden interpretations against what is told and recorded, and that is the second most important task of an oral history. I argue here that the scarcity of accounts by Black women about their lives renders what will follow original and extremely valuable. Within the narratives the women continually analyse the context of the politics of the time. To be Black in a predominantly white society, with all its incumbent difficulties, forces one constantly to evaluate experience against an active and external mechanism of subordination. That is, laws, rules, policy, attitudes, all designed to inhibit one's activities and aspirations, have to be responded to, so these analyses become part of how life is articulated; these laws, rules, policy, attitudes, etc., are the obstacles through which life is negotiated.

As a researcher, it also became apparent to me that much could be revealed by these women's experiences which could influence the approach of feminist research. Appraisal of work outside the home was perhaps the most important consideration in structuring the interview questions. I sought to examine work outside the home as a central theme in Black women's lives. For these women I knew — because they were women and because they were Black — work outside the home was imperative.

De facto segregation in Canada and its concomitant inequalities placed Black women in the early half of the century in an acutely difficult position; how were their daily lives, choices and aspirations structured?

An open-ended interview format was used, asking the women to tell about their childhood, how it was growing up in Canada in the early part of this century. I had developed a list of thirty questions which were to be the basis of the interviews.

The interviewer posed the "known" social history against the women's recollections — "When the war broke out what did the government say?" Or "How much was the price of bread in 1935?" Then there was the "unknown" social history. Because they were Black and women, questions such as "What were your wages?" "Where did you/Black people live?" "How did you have children and work?" "What was the 'community' like?" "Was there discrimination?" "How did you deal with this or that situation?" "Where did you all socialise?" "What kind of music did you dance to?" One woman responded laughing at me as if I ought to know better, "Oh jazz, dear!" Questions such as these dug up the everyday nature of Black life. The most important question was, "Did you work outside the home and what did you work at?" I would also ask the women to go through a day or a week of their life. What did they think of women's liberation and, lastly, all the interviewers would always ask if these women had any advice for younger women. One woman laughingly responded to another interviewer, "Stay away from love and evil men."

I was curious about Black experience in the country as a whole but even more curious about it from the point of view of Blacks who had lived here for generations. How did women live within communities so besieged? I wanted to recover the everyday detail of their lives, to ask them how it was, and what they did to survive. Being Black and a woman myself, but not being able to conceive of times without even the minimal gains of the Civil Rights movement of the 1960s, how they lived, and that how they lived had not been recorded were the primary factors motivating my inquiries. Only one woman in the narratives was born outside of Canada. Naturally, all of the interviewers were Black women, so at the beginning of the interviews there was an implicit understanding of being in something together. What we were in together was the condition of being Black women, a relation distinct from any other relation existing between people not of this group and distinct from relations with people outside of this group. We shared assessments, situations, methods of thought and patterns of the culture to which we belonged. There was an understanding that we were exploited. We were wronged together. That bond was the initial one. Within this, however, there were great complexities and contradictions: to name a few, class or class aspirations, education and positions on Black issues. For example, two women I interviewed challenged me on the Black Power movement, saying that it was destructive and that things were going fine for Black people before it came along and, furthermore, that it was a Caribbean-émigré-led movement. Then they asked me what I thought. Drawing the Marcus Garvey analogy in their case, I argued the significance of the Black Power movement to me at sixteen. In many ways, that heated point in the interview, where ideas were exchanged instead of absorbed into the tape, deepened the candour of the rest of the interview. Of course, the women wanted to know about me too, to situate me and my thoughts.

I think that I can say that the oral histories were seen by all of us, interviewers and interviewed, as one means in the effort to change our condition, but perhaps the most difficult hurdle was to surmount the notion that women could not speak as authorities. At least half of the women said at first that they had nothing substantial to say, but of course they did and their narratives are rich and insightful. I am deeply grateful for their generosity in sharing their experiences. I am convinced that if they had not told us we would not know about this past.

The title, *No Burden To Carry*, is borrowed from a woman not included in these narratives. In the 1930s her mother and father told her that education was "no burden to carry," and no one could take it away from her. It struck me that with this advice they might have felt that they were handing her a way out of both gender and race inequality. The subtitle, *Narratives of Black Working Women In Ontario 1920s–1950s*, is given because these narratives do not hope to, or claim to, cover the whole life of the women who tell them, hence they are narratives of a certain time, narratives of particular moments in history.

Notes

1. Joan Kelly, *Women, History and Theory* (London, University of Chicago Press, 1984), p. 2.

2. *Ibid.*, p. 3.

3. Deborah Gray White, *Ar'n't I a Woman? Female Slaves in the Plantation South.* (New York, W.W. Norton and Company, 1985) and Jacqueline Jones, *Labour of Love, Labour of Sorrow* (New York, Vintage Books, Random House, 1985).

4. Genevieve Leslie, "Domestic Service in Canada, 1880–20," in Janice Acton, Penny Goldsmith and Bonnie Sheppard, eds. *Women at Work: Ontario 1850–1930* (Toronto, Women's Press, 1974).

5. James St. G. Walker, *A History of Blacks in Canada: A Study Guide* (Ottawa, Ministry of State-Multiculturalism, 1981), p. 132.

6. Jones, *op. cit.*, p. 200.

7. Amy Jacques-Garvey, *Philosophy and Opinions of Marcus Garvey* (New York, Atheneum, 1923).

8. Robin W. Winks, *The Blacks in Canada: A History* (Montreal, New Haven and London, McGill-Queen's University Press and Yale University Press, 1971), p. 424.

9. *Ibid.*, p. 337.

10. *Ibid.*, p. 338.

11. *Ibid.*, p. 344.

12. Dorothy Sterling, *We Are Your Sisters* (New York, W.W. Norton & Company, 1984), p. 172.

13. Ruth Roach Pierson, *"They're Still Woman After All": The*

Second World War and Canadian Womanhood (Toronto, Mc-Clelland and Stewart Limited, 1986), p. 22.

14. Winks, *op. cit.*, pp. 420–423.

15. *Ibid.*, p. 423.

16. Pierson, *op. cit.*, p. 27.

17. *Ibid.*

18. *Ibid.*

19. Walker, *op. cit.*, p. 132.

20. Winks, *op. cit.*, p. 388.

21. Pierson, *op. cit.*, p. 32.

22. Pierson, *op. cit.*, p. 47.

23. Pierson, *op. cit.*, p. 61.

24. Jones, *op. cit.*, pp. 236–237.

25. Jones, *op. cit.*, p. 208.

26. Jones, *op. cit.*, p. 240.

27. Jones, *op. cit.*, p. 257.

28. Linda Martin and Kerry Segrave, *The Servant Problem* (North Carolina and London, McFarland & Company, 1985), p. 55.

29. Gayatri Spivak, "Three Women's Texts and a Critique of Imperialism," in Henry Louis Gates Jr., ed., *Race, Writing and Difference* (Chicago and London, The University of Chicago Press, 1986), p. 266.

30. *Ibid.*, p. 269.

Violet Blackman
1900–1990

We had was to come by boat and be landed in New York; then we took the train from New York to Toronto.

That was 1920; then Toronto was just a village. The streetcars had no sidings to them; you could jump on and off, but they always had the motorman and a conductor on them. The Exhibition Ground and Sunnyside, that was all the lake, and the Union Station — all there was nothing but the lake.

You couldn't get any position, regardless who you were and how educated you were, other than housework, because even if the employer would employ you, those that you had to work with would not work with you.

It was a man here — he's still here — Donald Moore. He saw the conditions, he formed a committee, and we used to go to different churches and hold different rallies. It was the '30s. Later, with this committee, he went to Ottawa with a brief and presented it — of allowing the coloured people from the different islands to come in.[1] Then, after that, the government permit that so many could come in each year from different islands. But you had to come in as a domestic: you had to go and serve a year with some lady up in Rosedale or up in the upper section, and then when you're satisfactory — took a year — you get your landing, and you're free to go and do anything that you want to do. That was how coloured people start coming into this country.[2]

But even then the barrier was there: you couldn't go to any of the hospitals to work, or the telephone company and all those different places. There were no nurses in the hospitals — no nothing there — because of colour; they wouldn't have you, even though lots of the people came here was quite qualified.

The honourable Marcus Garvey, he started in Jamaica; then he went to New York, and he start the movement of the Universal Negro Improvement Association (UNIA). A man came from there — he was a doctor, I forget his name now — he got a committee and opened a section.[3]

Marcus Garvey was coming here to have a convention and we couldn't really obtain a building; no one would rent. I knew the white people knew about Marcus Garvey even more than we, the coloured, did: they were afraid that he was coming here to stir up the coloured people, and so they planned to stop him at the border. But we had a lawyer here by the name of Pitt, and he was the one that went to have him cleared because they did stop Marcus Garvey from coming in.[4]

Lots of people didn't like Mr. Pitt, but he was a wonderful racial man. There was a lot of young Blacks that would've gone to jail hadn't been for Lawyer Pitt, and whether you had money, or whether you didn't have money, Lawyer Pitt just want to know that you were going to court, and he would be down there to defend you.[5] I don't think he even knew them. He just heard: my child is up for so and so — there used to be an awful lot of fights between the Jews and the Blacks, helluva fight. The poor Blacks have nobody, so Lawyer Pitt have to go down there, and the sentence it would be no time in jail, it would be bail. He was a marvellous lawyer, and he would never take the back seat to the white man. The white man did everything, every damn thing what to have something over this man, but he wouldn't take anything.

There was a minister here — Reverend Stewart from Jamaica — and he had a church over at Elm Street. It was Reverend Stewart that gave us the church was to hold the convention for Marcus Garvey. We had the convention, but the way Marcus Garvey wanted was to deliver to the Black people. He wasn't able to because there was police detectives all inside the building and outside the church — all over. It was clear then, within ourselves, we, the members of the UNIA, that we were going to buy a building and when he come back the next time, he would have his own building for him to have his convention. That's how the UNIA building on College Street were bought.[6]

At first, we were renting a building down on Queen Street right across from Augusta — that building is still there, they have a hardware store there now. The second time when Marcus Garvey came back here we had the building here, and he was able to hold his convention at that hall. On College, the UNIA had two floors there because we had our own orchestra, and every night of the week there was something. If you wanted to meet any coloured face at all, you had to go to the UNIA.

How we had the down payment, there was a man by the name of Bailey was the president then, and he had some little books that you go out and beg people to give you a donation. My God, I asked even the streetcar conductor! And these little books was given out to the members — there was a prize to be given out to the one that brought in the most. My collection was five hundred dollars. At that time that was plenty of money. I was working in service then; when I got my day off I used to go to all the homes in the surroundings where I was working and those people was very generous. The lady that I was working for — and there was herself, her husband and her sister — and they gave me quite a bit, even knowing what the occasion was for.

I can't remember when the UNIA was formulated, but I remember a friend came to where I was working in service — after I was here a year — and invited me this Sunday to go down to the UNIA, and when I went I liked it very much and I joined. From then I became an active member — I never missed a Sunday — and I worked with it. I was in everything. At that time I had a voice; I was in the choir — I was in everything in the UNIA 'cause I liked it all my life once I got in there and saw how interesting it was.

They had everything: they had their own brass band, they had a choir, they used to put on plays, different plays, and we had even a Prince from Africa came. And it was wonderful, wonderful! This is why I put all my labour, all my time in it.

We start paying for the building then and the building was paid off. We bought a beautiful chair, the Marcus Garvey chair. The history behind that chair is it's the chair that we bought for Marcus Garvey when we first moved into the building. I don't know who has that chair; I had it, but I hadn't found a place to keep it. I'm sorry I gave it up.

And that's what hurt me the most — when they sell off the building — because our main object was there were the younger people that was coming up, and we hoped that they would have something that they was proud of and something that they could call their own. We rallied with that building!

There was children's programme every Sunday, different ones. Mrs. Mercury and myself was in charge of the programmes for the children. It was nothing because different ones of the younger set that was old enough to conduct it, they would build up. You gave them up the chance to build up a programme and conduct it, and they used to do that.

We used to have different recitals, socials. We had everything that you could ever think of: we had dinners; we had dances — there was nothing that you lacked coming there. Every day of the week there was something going on up in the UNIA.

We had the ladies. We had a committee — I formed a committee — and each lady was responsible for either putting on a dinner or putting on a social, putting on a dance. We didn't work like individuals. When any of the ladies are putting on anything I work with them just equally because that's the only way you can work with people — my people especially, don't feel you're above them because you hold a position — so we all was responsible, and though I was the chairlady, anything I did had to go to the heads, to the president or the treasurer, and then I would come back to the committee. I was responsible for the things that goes on and for the money that is being made, and then I'd take it to the association. I worked hands and heart. Most of the things was prepared at my place; they would come there, and we all would share equally, and we got along nicely, wonderful. I miss all those things — the UNIA was my heart and my soul and my life.

We had such a hard time, the coloured people. The

UNIA after we bought it, all the different lodges used to come because they couldn't get any other places. They used to come to the UNIA to rent and things like that. Then no sooner the white world open, they can go in, they leave the UNIA, and we wouldn't be asking them half what the whites asking them because they had to pay for going in, whatever it is.

When Marcus Garvey came back the second time, we even learned more then about the movement. That was the time that we knew that he was going to launch his ship, Black Sta: Lines. A lot of us bought shares in it. He was so proud of his people, he didn't want the white man to have anything to do with it. He want from the firemen up to the heads just to be Black, but in the meantime they was selling him out.

He went to Liberia and saw all this rubber and all this money that the white man was making out of it, and he thought that if they can make it, why shouldn't who that it really concern make it? That was how he started selling shares and having the ship going there and importing rubber. But in the meantime, his Black people were selling him out to the white man: the first voyage that the Black Star Line made cost that man so much money! It's a wonder that no one died; that boat was deliberately run into a reef. It looked like an accident, but it was supposed to be that 'cause that got them running from the white man. Then coming back again he was took in prison in that Atlanta jail, Atlanta, Georgia. They expect him was to die.

He was very careful what he says when he go to give his lectures or anything like that, that the white man wouldn't have anything on him; everything was done in secret.

The thing came out that three times he was dead. He

was terrible sick down there and developed asthma and everything; he was supposed to die, but he didn't. God was with him and he didn't. But he came out. And up to now, I don't know whether Marcus Garvey is dead or not — he supposed to be dead. He went to England, and they said that they'd poisoned him, I don't know how true that is.

Now that church at Shaw Street, all of us as members of the UNIA have money in that church. It was Reverend Stewart who had the plans for the church at Shaw Street. He's dead and gone, but it was Reverend Stewart who caused them to have that church here today. When the building where he had his church was sold, Reverend Stewart came to us and we had the empty second floor. It wasn't rented then, and we gave Reverend Stewart that hall to hold his services until he was able to obtain a church. It was while he was there holding his services that he saw this church was up for sale. He went in and intercede, to see if he could get it — which he was lucky. Now he got it, but he didn't have the amount of money for the down payment that they were asking.

He came back to us and told us what was happening, and everyone of us that was there donated so much money at the time that he could go and make the down payment, and we pledged to pay so much a week. I know I pledge fifty dollars — that was a lot of money — and every Saturday morning Reverend Stewart was at my place to collect what I was giving. We all have money in that church on Shaw Street, and it was Reverend Stewart who start buying that building.

The Nova Scotia people who got there today have to thank Reverend Stewart that they're here. Reverend Stewart heard about the conditions of the Black people down in Nova Scotia and made the trip down there; when he went down there, he saw that it was, exactly what they said it was, and he came back, he took up a collection, and he send down to help. He went up to Rosedale, and he had as many ladies as he could get a hold of to send down and bring out girls to work in the homes, and while they were here, they sent back and helped their family to come out. And that's how the Nova Scotians start coming out from Nova Scotia here to Toronto — it was Reverend Stewart.

There was a man that came from England — I can't remember his name — he and Mr. Hutchinson and Mr. Laws, they couldn't get any other places where the white people was concerned. They heard about the UNIA, and they came here and asked if we would let them play dominoes there twice a week. The other members was very concerned about turning it into a gambling place and they object.

A meeting was called of officers — I was one of them at the time — and they were against it terrible. I interceded, and I told them that after all the Universal Negro Improvement Association identified that regardless of where you're from, you have a chance of coming in until you improve yourself. We said we'll give them a tryout and see what happen — if they want to turn it into a gambling session, then we would have to let them go. They came in and they were all right. At that time the UNIA didn't have very many members.

There was another man here at the UNIA by the name of Mr. Davis — nobody hears of Mr. Davis now. He was the one who brought the credit union. Reverend Stewart was holding his church services then — all of us was at that service — but Mr. Davis had to go to a meeting; it was to do with the firm that he was working for. When he got there, he learned about this credit union because they had a credit union.

He came back to the meeting and told us what he learned about this credit union; he thought that it would be a very good thing for the Black people. My husband, Mr. Blackman, was here then, and we went up to the Parliament Buildings; they said you had to have twelve to form a committee and we came back — Reverend Stewart was there, and Lawyer Pitt and another minister as was at the AME (African Methodist Episcopal) church — and we formed a committee.

We had a hard time, but we did obtain the charter and we formed the credit union. That credit union was marvellous. Lots of people bought their homes out of that credit union. My husband was president for twelve years.

Later it start going downhill, until the credit union was in so much debt that the league of credit unions said we couldn't top a rate. Bad management. I think it was sixty thousand dollars debt that they had to carry, and the credit union league had to carry our credit, so they said they either had to fold up or either come up with the money. That was how we lose our credit union. We could have been something that the world could look upon today.

And we're grudgeful: we don't want to see anyone get ahead; we do our damnedest to pull them down instead of putting them ahead like the other nationalities. The other nationalities have their misunderstandings, but they're willing to help one another to get up there. We pull down. We could have been a monument here today. I'm very happy to see how the younger people is coming up now — they are trying to make up for lost time. But we could have been so much; we could've had places that our young people could go and do things, improve themselves.

When the UNIA was sold I took sick, because that was one building where I felt within myself that, even if I'm gone from here, my young children that was twenty up could open that door, and no one could tell them that they can't come in. But they have nothing now; what have they got that they can say: I can go to this hall; I can go this building and they can't refuse having me there?

We need to do something for the young people to encourage them and to give them something to hold on to, something that they can look up to. They're happy now with Black History Week and things like that which they've never had before. They're learning now they can get books on the history of the Black people in the past to show them that their nationalities and their foreparents did do something. Before, even this was hidden from them: they were ignorant of the fact of what their foreparents has done. That's why I think the Black people look up to the white people like their superior: it was everything the white people; the Black people never did anything because it was all hidden. Now it is coming out, now that we can go to the library and get books and read up on it. They have Black History Week and things like that. Little by little — it will take a long time though, it will take a long time.

After the UNIA building was sold, Mr. Laws was renting a place on Vaughan. That didn't achieve anything either, just rode up into a whole lot of expense. I think the building was sold for 250,000 dollars. I think that two hundred was going for debts against the building — and there were three floors! They were getting 680 dollars for the two rooms — and there was another second floor and then there was a third floor. I am telling you it's pathetic: there is nothing functioning now as far as the UNIA is concerned; it is just out of existence.

At Portland and Queen there is a soldier that is there, a great big statue, a beautiful statue, of a Black man. He gave his life to save his whole battalion. At the City Hall they have the records there of him. But what I am against is all those statues are on University and that man is put away there at Portland and Queen; I'm damn sure he did more than those people who are there — he sacrificed his life.

Mr. Moore used to have a parade every year on that day that they have for soldiers to end the war with, and we used to look forward to it. The parade went from the UNIA: go down to Spadina, walk on Spadina to Queen, turn west of Queen till we come to Bathurst and turn south of Bathurst to this park: that was a first time I saw that beautiful statue. You used to have all the officials from the City Hall come. You used to have a regular picnic: you'd bring your picnic basket and all the tables, and all these men would give their different speeches. Mrs. Holloway — she had a son that was killed in the war — she used to place the wreath at the foot of that man. Since Mr. Moore stopped, nothing is said about that man anymore, and I think that we as Black people should honour him.

Now I'm damned sure that if it was the other nationalities, that statue wouldn't have been stuck back there in that park, it would have been on University. And we, all the Black people who are here, should see to it that he's moved from here and put with the others. If our children coming see that statue, they would stop and think and say: he did something. They don't know because they don't even know he was there; he's dead and gone, but he saved the battalion.

I have to mention there's a few other women that have gone on that were with the UNIA. There's Mrs. Sobers, she was one of the committee. All these women. There is Mrs. Edith Holloway, Mrs. Braithwaite — Danny's mother and father. All those people gave their time. Mrs. Barkely, Mrs.

Davis, Mrs. Ethel Wynn — all those people are people I have worked with.

There are so much advantages here now. When I was sending my two girls to school there wasn't the advantages as now. My oldest girl I can remember as anything. When she was graduating from public school to go to high school she wanted me to send her to the technical school, but I says, "No. You go to collegiate schools and the best ones."

And she says, "What if I'd come out and there won't be anything because they won't take me?" And I says, "Listen, it's not going to be like this all the time. The door is going to be open one day. You make damn sure that when that door swings back, you have what to walk through. We cannot be standing outside and saying, 'If I had known.' " I said, "If I had to take you and clap your behind down in one of these chairs in the collegiate, you go."

Parkdale, having been the most outstanding collegiate then, she went to that collegiate. She and another fellow, Brooks, was the only two coloured people that was in there. And so say, it was the same thing happen: I wanted her to go to the university. When she graduated from Parkdale, one morning she says, "Mother, sit down. I want to talk to you." And right then I felt that something was up. She said, "I have a foundation now that I can build anything that I want to build. What I want you to do for me is to let me go to a business college and I can build anything from there."

I cried all that night. In the morning it was just like something said to me: listen to her and send her to a business college. Dominion Business College was the outstanding business college then and I send her to there. At that time the barrier was breaking: they didn't care who you are; you had what they want, that was it. They didn't stop to think of the colour: it was just what they want and have it. And that was it.

The only advice that I could give to the young people is: regardless what the barriers may be, just keep on going; if you have it in you, just go on; and if there's a way that you can give a helping hand to the next one that isn't as fortunate as you are, please stretch the hands and leave it for them.

I never stopped to think of myself. I'd think of knowing that I'd be helping somebody, and if it hadn't been I had stretched the hands of compassion, that person could have been not fulfilling what they were able or capable of doing. There are the many today who would've gone back home and wouldn't have had the chance, if I didn't open my door for them at the time; the opportunity was there, but if they weren't in a position to obtain it, they'd have to sit by or go on back home, bury up the talent that they had, that God gave to them, just for a little help. Thanks be to Almighty God, every one of those young men is out there measuring themselves man among men. It was hard, but I'm here, and they're out there doing the things that they enjoy, the things that they came here for. One of my boys is a millionaire today. Denham and Horace, they started with me.

All of those people have done so much, they should have a hall now. That's what I hope when I'm praying: have a whole side with all the pictures of those people who have done things and then gone on; our names would be there, and our children would come in and ask and would read and see the names. But what have we got to show our children? What have we got? They just have to come up and scratch the ground. That's what bothers me.

I'm eighty-eight now, eighty-eight last Sunday, going on

my eighty-nine now, and I have no regrets. The only regrets I have is to know I couldn't do anything at that time about the UNIA because my husband was sick on my hands.

Notes

1. In April 1954, Donald Moore, then president of the Negro Citizens' Association, led a delegation to Ottawa, the first to meet with Cabinet about discrimination against West Indian immigration. See Winks, *op. cit.*, p.425. Before this only a trickle of West Indian immigrants had been allowed into Canada. Women who came earlier, like Violet Blackman, worked at what was called "indenture."

2. "Coloured" means West Indians here.

3. The UNIA started in Toronto in 1919. The first president was Abraham Thomas, an optician. Marcus Mosiah Garvey began the UNIA and what came to be known as Garveyism in Jamaica on August 1, 1914. Under the motto "One God! One Aim! One Destiny!" Garvey intended to unite "all the Negro peoples of the world into one great body to establish a country and government absolutely their own."

   Strongly influenced by Booker T. Washington and committed to ameliorate the conditions of Black people he had seen in the Caribbean, Latin America, England, the United States and Canada, Garvey said, "I asked: Where is the Black man's government? Where is his King and Kingdom? Where his President, his country, and his ambassador, his army, his navy, his men of big affairs? I could not find them and then I declared I will help to make them." The UNIA was modelled on these precepts, hence the Army and the Black Cross nurses, etc. The movement spread all over the United States and Canada, with a branch in Harlem in 1917 boasting 2,000 members. The Toronto branch began in 1919. For more information on the Garvey movement, see *Philosophy and Opinions of Marcus Garvey*, edited by Amy Jacques-Garvey (New York, Atheneum, 1973).

4. According to Danny Braithwaite, Garvey visited Toronto in 1925, 1936 and 1938. The UNIA held its annual conventions in Canada after Garvey was deported from the U.S. for alleged mail fraud. Winks, in *The Blacks in Canada*, says that Garvey was deported from Montreal in 1928, before he could fulfil speaking engagements in Ontario. Garvey is reported to have urged U.S. voters to vote against Herbert Hoover in the upcoming U.S. presidential election; the U.S. consul in Montreal protested to the Canadian government and Garvey was deported before moving on to Ontario. The 1936 International Conventions (sic) of the Negro Peoples of the World was held in Toronto in 1936 with Garvey presiding. See Winks, pp. 414–416.

5. According to Danny Braithwaite, B.J. Spencer Pitt led the UNIA in the 1930s and 1940s. According to Winks, Pitt "held the Toronto chapter of the UNIA together into the 1940s...." See Winks, *op. cit.*, p. 416.

6. Later the UNIA changed its name to the UAIA, the Universal African Improvement Association, and bought the building at 355 College Street, where it operated until 1982.

Addie Aylestock
1909

I was born here, my parents and my grandparents too. For a while there was only one other Black family around where we were living. I remember when I was quite young, my mother use to take four of us to Sarnia to visit an aunt there, and we would go on a boat and picnic. We went to Belle Isle — it was like a resort — and we would meet a lot of Black people. I do not know how far away it was from Sarnia, but I was amazed to see so many Black people. Then when I got older and came to Toronto I was more amazed.

My father was born in Ontario too, in Kitchener. Kitchener was Berlin when my father was born there, but because of the First World War they changed the name.[1]

I remember my grandmother, my mother's mother, but none of the others. She was very nice, very jovial. She had seventeen brothers and sisters, with one set of twins. She had a big farm, out in the country in what they call Peel Township. I used to like to go and stay with her on the farm, but my sister next to me didn't ever want to go. After she got older, the family had gone and I used to go and visit — the others were all away and married with their families. I was always willing to go; I guess that's why I'm alone now. Then my grandmother sold the farm, and she went to visit her different relatives, my aunts and uncles. I remember she used to come and spend some time at our place, I was always so pleased. She was seventy-two when she died, but she didn't have any grey hair.

I was born in the village Glen Allan, near Elmira, in 1909. It was a very small village, mostly farmers around there, and my dad worked for a farmer who had lots of cows. First of all, he helped to build a bridge, near Glen Allan. Then he was working at a furniture factory in Elmira; he walked back and forth at the end of the week. Then he got tired of that — there were farmers right around where we were living, just outside the village — so he started to work for a farm there. The farmers had quite a number of cows.

I think I was about eight years old when I started school, public school, in Glen Allan. The schools there usually have one or two rooms and there they had two rooms. I don't remember so much about there because shortly after I started school there, they removed to another village, a larger village about ten miles away to Drayton, and I was there for about three or four years.

My parents were moving quite a bit — and now I am older, I move quite a bit. It was usually work that made them move, usually work. There was some kind of a factory — I think it was a flax mill in Drayton — and there was more work there, and my dad decided to go there because there was more opportunity over there.

There was just one or two rooms in the school — I never went to a large school. We got to know each other well. At that time we were the only Black family going. There were eight of us and there were three going to school.

We did not have a farm in Glen Allan or Drayton. Later on when we moved, my dad did a little bit of farming, but there was a very small village. We children did just our gardening, and we helped to pull the weeds out and things like that.

Drayton was a small town; there were lots of conveniences there. I was the oldest of eight. There was not much to do. We had two teachers, one for each room in the school. I don't remember how many scholars there were, but I do remember there were a fair amount, about thirty or forty in each room. How did it feel to be the only Black in the school? We did not know any different; we didn't notice any difference. We were just brought up in that environment, that neighbourhood. Maybe some new ones would look at you kind of funny, but that was all.

After Drayton we moved to Lebanon. I called it the Cedar of Lebanon, referred to in the Bible, because there were cedar trees along the side of the house.

Again we moved because of employment. A cousin of mine had quite a big farm and quite a big business at Lucan. Before we went to Lucan, it was Lebanon. I think my dad went there again because of employment. The factory in Drayton had closed. My dad was a very hard-working man, he had a family — and there wasn't unemployment insurance then — and he felt where ever the opportunity was he would be there. Next we moved to Lebanon, again a small village, near Listowel.

I liked it there, but it was just the one-room school. We stayed there for a very short time. In fact, I tried my entrance there — a grade to get into high school. I did very well. I remember my mother was quite sick — at the time she was sick with pneumonia, and I had to miss school to stay home and help her — but I did very well. There was another young girl in my class — and we were both competing against one other and trying to get ahead of one another — and when we had our exams we both had the same marks.

Sometimes I had to miss school. My parents didn't feel they could send me to high school — high school was free then; it was a public school. But then there weren't many opportunities for Black girls anyway. I got an opportunity of going and staying at my aunt in Sarnia for a while. I was there for about a year. I just lived with her; then I got the idea that I wanted to work. My sister next to me come to Toronto, and so I got the idea that I wanted to work in Toronto too, so I asked my mother and dad. There was four of us — four girls. It seemed like we had the idea in our head to leave. Most of us left home pretty early because our parents were poor and weren't able to look after us.

My sister was doing domestic work, getting her room and board. And there was a friend, in the BME (British Methodist Episcopal) Church, of my mother's and my sister's.[2] When I came to Toronto I used to spend a lot of time at her home, so she sort of was chaperoning us. I was not quite sixteen.

Toronto was like a big city to me then, but not near as big as now. You can't compare: it wasn't built up like it is now. The city was three- or four-storey houses — I thought that was high!

I just came to Toronto for a short time, and then my friend in Stratford thought it would be nice for me to be there, so I went there for a little while — it was closer to home. I didn't think that that was really what I wanted, so I came back to Toronto.

When I worked as a domestic I didn't have much to do. I just got up and got out — got my breakfast and got out in the morning — and back at two o'clock in the afternoon, and then I got the dinner ready.

I think they gave me enough for carfare — I really don't remember, but it wasn't very much. I know when I first came to Toronto there weren't many opportunities for Black girls, in those days anyways. And then again, my parents were satisfied that I had a job in housework that I would stay in. I think I got fifteen dollars a month at the start — that was supposed to be enough for your clothes and your carfare. I lived in the west end of Toronto then, on Brighton Avenue.

I guess the Depression started when I came here to Toronto. It didn't really seem like a Depression to me. The reason I knew about the Depression was that I heard mother and dad talking about it. I didn't realize that's what it was, but I knew that sometimes we were getting the same thing to eat, like beans, turnips, maybe something the farmers would give us. My parents didn't have money to go out and buy much.

I started dressmaking at an evening class at the Central Tech here in Toronto. When I was going to class I'd see all these people coming from the Toronto Bible College, and I felt that maybe that was what the Lord wanted me to do instead of dressmaking, although I had gone to dressmaking for almost three years and was almost ready to get a diploma. I had got the first and second year. So I prayed about it and I felt that's what the Lord wanted me to do. I changed and started to go to the Bible college.

In the meantime, I had already got interested in the BME church in Toronto, which was on Chestnut street there, and it was quite active — the young people and Sunday school work. The pastor of the church, who was also the superintendent of the BME Conference of Churches, suggested that I become a deaconess of the conference. That meant that I would go and assist the minister, or maybe go to another neighbouring church, see if there was help needed and stay there a little bit. I thought if I could be of greater service, I thought maybe I would do it.

I was quite active. I had become quite active in the church, the BME church, when I was still quite young. The BME church came out of the AME — the African Methodist Episcopal Church. It was all one, and the AME had their headquarters in the United States. The Canadian people that had joined the church, they felt that they wanted a headquarters in Canada, and at that time they were collecting money and sending it over to the States. Their assessments, and so on, went to supporting a bishop over there in the States, and they felt they wanted their headquarters in Canada, so they sent in their resolution to the conference, asking for permission to set up a separate church, which they did. This happened around 1856.

They had the first conference in Chatham. At first they were going to call it "Canadian Methodist Episcopal" because they're in Canada, but then they decided to call it "British" because they got freedom under the British flag, under Queen Victoria. I guess the conference — when they started making the BME — didn't seem to realize the importance of keeping a record, and then some of the records they had they were lost. They were put in a vault in a bank there in Windsor, and apparently something happened, and nobody seemed to know what happened. About twenty years ago, they went to this vault and there was nothing there — just some little papers that didn't amount to anything. Several in the church have started to write the history, but right now I don't think there is anything finished of the BME. There is something finished of the AME of the States, but not the BME. It is a pity.

I was interested in the young people, in the Sunday school work, and usually attended the prayer meetings. I really enjoyed church work. I took the course sponsored by the church. It was the training we needed, so I decided to go to the Bible college. I just went for one year. Then I had an idea the Lord wanted me to go to mission work, and I didn't feel that I wanted to wait very long. I thought I'd just take the one-year course and they didn't object. But then I started on as a deaconess and I kept building. I really needed more qualifications.

First of all, when I went to the Bible college they gave me another year of high school. At that time they had what they called the "prep year," and they gave me another year of the high school to get a better foundation. There were quite a number that were older that were taking this course that hadn't finished their high school work.

In the regular course they had other classes, which were about the same as you'd get every year at the high school. At that time there weren't so many as were finishing high school and going on to university, but now, of course, that's a qualification you need to go to Bible college. I took that and then I graduated there in '45.

When I came to finish up I remember there were quite a number of students at the Bible college that had started then, but they had to go because of the Depression. There was more employment later then, of course, because of the war. It's regretful that there was more employment because of the war — then there seemed to be more Blacks in the city too, because of opportunities, more employment. But I don't know of any particular change otherwise. When I started my Bible studies the Bible college was on Spadina near Bloor. The job that I got after was in the north end of the city, so I used to take Yonge and transfer to go to Spadina — they tore down that Bible college. I went to it for one year, and then I went back again for two years. Took a three year course.

I took a missionary medical course when I had the idea of going to Africa. I had Liberia in mind. Since then I have met some from Liberia and explained the Christian way. They said you don't have to learn a different language.

When I went to the medical institute I felt I needed some type of special training. There was an urgent call for teachers, so I did a short nursing course. I remember I used to assist: I would come down to the Salvation Army that was on Bloor Street then and help there in the mornings and go back to the school in the afternoon to take the course. I enjoyed it too. I'm still serious about the church.

I don't think there was anything else about Africa that made me want to go there. I had just seen all kinds of pictures, heard missionaries talk about it, and I felt that there's plenty over here to help the people, and I should be willing to go over there and help the people in Africa.

First of all, I was made a deaconess of the conference, a consecrated deaconess of the conference of '44. Then in '45 I graduated from the Toronto Bible College. The superintendent of the conference asked me if I would be willing to go and assist at the church in Halifax, so I was there about a year.

I really enjoyed it there. I told him, when he just asked me, "Well, I feel the Lord wants me to do mission work." And I said, "I feel I want to go to Africa. The Lord wants me to go to Africa." He says, "You'll get all the Africa you want!" — and, of course, there was a part there called Africville, settled back of Halifax.[3]

I knew that Black people had set up a whole community, Africville. There was a lot of opposition about Africville because the city officials wanted to rearrange the way they were. I don't know as there's a difference between Halifax people and Toronto people: the people in Africville preferred their old way instead of the new way, but there's so many things that has to be destroyed before you get the new way. The church then was right downtown on Falkland Street.

I assisted the minister, who lived right in Halifax. At the time we had a BME church there, and I assisted there with the service and with the Sunday school work. Then in the week he would go up there visiting and I'd go with him. It was quite different, of course, but I felt that was where the Lord wanted me to go, and I really enjoyed it. It was like a pioneer place because they had their animals and everything in one building. They did enjoy getting together for church. They see us coming, they'd leave everything — they wouldn't bother wash, or change, or anything — they'd just come to church. It was like the hymn *Just As I Am*. But really they appreciated it, so I enjoyed that. I was just there a little over a year when they decided to bring me back, and then I went to Montreal.

They were trying to reorganize the church there. They had a BME church there several years ago. I understand the ministers weren't getting enough salary or something and they went back to the States — they could get more there.

After I was in Montreal for over a year, they appointed another minister in Montreal. He had been in the conference a long time ago and had gone to the States, but he decided he wanted to come and finish his days over here, so the superintendent sent word that the minister was coming.

He happened to be my second cousin, the Reverend Lawson. So we worked together for a while and were trying to get a church. We were renting at the UNIA Hall there for the services on Sunday, and I had quite a group of young people — a mission band that met in the week. We were doing very well, and then he decided he didn't want to continue on. The conference wasn't sending him enough money. Of course, he had been getting big money in the States. So the conference time came, he had his trunk packed and he wasn't going back again.

The church up and closed — and now they were trying to get reorganized — and they asked me if I would go down and do visitation work. So I did and I was there one year when another deaconess, who had just recently been consecrated in the conference, had married a minister, so they were sent there. I was told they didn't need me there when the deaconess and the minister were there 'cause the other lady was doing the deacon's work, so I came back again to Toronto. For my vacation I'd go home where my parents were.

I wasn't exactly paid a salary as a deaconess. They'd give me something to keep me going. That was all, just enough to keep me going. Now when I was in Halifax they didn't pay anything — they just sent something to the minister there — and they'd see that I'd get a little room and a little food. And people there would bring in something for the family and, of course, they'd share. The conference would give me a little bit maybe every two or three months, but there wasn't really a salary. I never did go into salary.

When I was a deaconess I'd go and help with the young peoples' work, the Sunday school work, and maybe teach or do some visiting in the homes because the ministers in those days — in fact, some even now are working at other jobs — they didn't have much time for visitation. I would do the visitation — people who were attending church and those who weren't attending. And then I went to assist with the prayer meeting or whatever meetings they were having during the week. Sunday, we'd agreed that I would read the Scriptures, offer a prayer. When I was a pastor — I still wasn't ordained — I would hold the services, do the speaking and do the everything else. I could serve the communion, but I couldn't consecrate the elements.

Then after I went back to Toronto, the conference met in London. A minister was appointed to Owen Sound and he hadn't been very well. They said it was very cold in Owen Sound and he said he wasn't going. Of course, we're supposed to go where we're sent, but he said he wasn't going to Owen Sound. He walked out of the church; he wouldn't even take the appointment. Then the superintendent said he'd like me to go. I still wasn't ordained; I was still a deaconess. But then, of course, you could assist in the churches; you could do mostly anything but marry people and things like that.

I was sent to Owen Sound and I did very well there. They seemed to like me and I got along very well. And the superintendent — he happened to be the pastor of the Toronto church — he would come up maybe once a month or every other month to assist with what was necessary, particularly with the communion service. But then he was the one who put in the resolution to ordain women — 'cause he felt I had a very important position and I was doing the same work as the men were doing. And I had also got the training — in those days they didn't feel it was urgent to go on to university. He put a resolution in to the general conference and it was passed.

It was 1950 when the resolution was put in and in 1951

I was ordained. A recommendation that was presented to the conference, the conference either had to reject or pass. Reverend Jackson, Reverend T.H. Jackson, he was the one that said I should be ordained. There were just one or two, I think, that objected at the time.

Then I was sent back to Owen Sound for a year or two and then I was stationed. I did everything. I felt quite excited. Sometimes I really felt I wasn't capable in a way, and I thought, well Lord, you've already been using me to do about the same thing. But somehow I was thankful and grateful, but I wasn't proud. Some people would say, "Oh, you're the first woman, the only woman!" 'Cause at that time there wasn't any other women. I'm the first Black woman that we know of to be a pastor in Canada.

There were two or three other women pastors that were living in Canada — one in the Baptist Church, and then there was one in the AME, but she told me she had to go into the States to get further in the service. She told me they wouldn't do that in Canada; they didn't believe that in the Canadian churches, but if you went over there and came back to Canada after, then you could be a woman pastor. But as far as I know I'm the first Black woman ordained in a church in Canada. I know I was the first with the BME. In fact, right now I'm the only one. There was this other one that was a deaconess, and she persuaded them to ordain her because of her services and so on, but then she passed away a few years afterwards. So I'm the only one right now.

In Owen Sound there were two or three white families that lived close to the church that came, but the others were Black. We always tried to make it known that it was for everybody, but so many when they see the Black people go to the church, they think it's just for the Blacks. But in each church we have a few of the others that come; the church is for all.

The reason we have the Black church is because of some discrimination. But we do find that sometime there are a few that wonder why others in our church are white, and I say the church is for all, for who ever will come. And that's the way it is.

In Owen Sound we had a very small number of people coming to church for most of the year because the men — and some of the women too — were sailors and they went out most of the year sailing on the boats. But then in the winter they'd be home, and they would cooperate, but they sent financial support, which was, of course, much smaller than it would be now, but the cost of living was lower too. I enjoyed it there.

In 1951 I went to North Buxton the first time. I went there for eight and a half years, and then I was sent to Guelph, but I wasn't there very long — I think about a year — and then I was sent to St. Catharines and then from St. Catharines to Niagara Falls and Fort Erie.

It was about three years that I was in Owen Sound, and then I went to North Buxton. I was there eight and a half years first; then I went back there again for another two years. North Buxton is a rural district, mostly all Black people, and I lived right across from the church, by the cemetery. Mother and Dad had moved to Lucan in the meantime. It was lonely at times. I was in the country. Sometimes I was alone there in a six-room house and all I had in the house was a cat. But on the other hand, until I came to Toronto, I was accustomed to small places, though not quite as isolated as North Buxton. It seemed like home in North Buxton because I was born in a small place; the people were so friendly, and they were always gracious.

At first when I came I didn't get very much salary. But because the farmers around there always had plenty of food — plenty of eggs and milk and vegetables and fruit — everybody was always bringing me something, and I certainly appreciated that too. But the best thing is that many are still doing for the Lord and carrying on the work. The salary wasn't much because the farmers weren't getting very much for their produce then. They had to wait a certain time of the year to get the little bit of money. But they were good at seeing that I was taken care of because they'd bring me produce — chickens and the meat from the pigs and the cows. Of course, for a while I had a very nice garden. When I was moved to different places perhaps I would get a little offering. It wasn't a salary, but it was just a little offering, and you had to manage on that offering. Sometimes it'd be quite a bit and sometimes it'd be very little. I thank the Lord that he did give me the grace. Somehow I knew he would still provide some way.

I wasn't driving at the time and it was very difficult. I found that was a necessity after I got to North Buxton. When you went to shop there was a small store in North Buxton, but if you wanted anything in particular, you had to go to Chatham, which was eight miles away. There was a bus there and I could grab it back and forth from Chatham, but in North Buxton there was only a short distance I could walk out there. And also the people who became ill were in hospitals in Chatham, so you also had to go there, and sometimes it was difficult to get somebody to take you because they were mostly all farmers around me. So I decided I better drive — and the different ones in Owen Sound was telling me I should drive.

I learned to drive in North Buxton. I used to drive back and forth to Chatham and Windsor and then to London and different places. I enjoyed driving. And then after I was in St. Catharines — I was there about three years — I was appointed to Windsor. But the minister there didn't want to leave and I still stayed in St. Catharines.

At that time my dad had passed, and my mother was living with me, and she didn't like moving around a lot neither. So we stayed in St. Catharines, and on the weekends I commuted back and forth to Windsor. Then the superintendent, who was again the pastor in Toronto, Reverend Markham, he went to Windsor for a while, and I went to Toronto. I was in charge of the Toronto church for, I think, about two or three months. Then he decided to turn it around again, and he came back to this meeting and persuaded this other minister to take over Windsor. For a while I was just visiting different churches, assisting. I had sort of a year off.

In our conference we're supposed to go where we're sent. Of course, sometimes now some of the ministers prefer to remain where they are because of jobs. I remember one time the minister wanted me to go back to North Buxton, and I felt it was a turn for somebody else to go. He said he couldn't send them a different minister. I referred to different ones that had been in places so long — many years — and he said he didn't want to move them — these men ministers — because they either had a family or a good job. I said, "I'll have to get a good job or get married!" He said, "Do the latter!"

So I was in Windsor twice. I went to Windsor then for just a very short time. Then I was sent back to Windsor and I was in Windsor when I retired. In fact, I had also had Chatham and part of the time I was in North Buxton. After I retired I moved to Windsor.

I had been in Windsor, I think, about two or three years,

and then I asked to be relieved of pastoral duties. At that time I was the pastor and I was also the general secretary of the conference of Churches. I was general secretary for twenty-four years. I wasn't very well for a while and I asked to be relieved of the pastoral duty. But I was still general secretary, so I got an apartment and lived in Windsor, and then afterwards, I asked also to be relieved of the secretary duty. I really was supposed to be retired in 1980, but I still lived in Windsor for a while.

I retired from the pastoral duties in 1980, but then I continued on with the secretary duties for another two years. And at that time I took a sick spell at the Conference, so I'd already told them that I wasn't going to take the position anymore, that I felt it was time for somebody else. I felt that it was necessary for me to be relieved, so in that two years, in 1982, I retired from general secretary at the general conference.

Still, I assisted in Windsor for a short time. My sister and one of my brothers and her niece and nephew came to visit me, and they suggested that since I was retired, I should get me a home closer to them, and that's why I'm in Scarborough now.

When I came to Scarborough I thought I would be attending the BME church downtown, which is on Shaw Street now, but it's quite a distance away. Then, in the meantime, they already had started this church at East York which is a branch of the BME. It was closer, so I decided I would go there. And then after I started there, of course, the minister there asked me to assist. So I was assisting again. He passed away in February, so then I have been pastor and out of retirement again.

We usually make all decisions at the conference. Right now we only have churches in Ontario. For a while there,

there was one in Halifax, Nova Scotia, and there was one in Winnipeg and in Montreal, Quebec, but now we just have churches in Ontario. There's eleven churches in Ontario.

I guess I was just gradually brought up in the church, although it wasn't the church that I am in now. It was Methodist and a white church. I guess the Lord had his hand on me when I was quite young. Quite young I felt the Lord wanted me to do something in particular, but I didn't know what it was.

When we were quite young my mother wasn't very active in the church, but both mother and dad always wanted us to go to church and Sunday school. They'd have us get up and get ready for Sunday school — and they were quite strict compared to what they are today because when we came home from church or Sunday school, we couldn't go outside and play around. We pretended we were in Sunday school again and played Sunday school and being the teacher and so forth. We went along. We weren't allowed to go out and play ball — like they are now — and all them sports.

And then as we got a little older, as my younger sisters and brothers got older, my mother started coming. She enjoyed the church and she always encouraged us in the church. My dad used to attend church quite regular too; then as he got older, he didn't seem to have the same desire. But mother became quite active; by the time we had moved to Lucan, near London, she became quite active in the women's group there. But again, it was the United Church.

There is a women's section in our church. Mother was quite active in it — it was called the Women's Auxiliary — and she used to attend the meetings. Once a month, I think it was. They would have socials and she was always baking for them: she enjoyed cooking, enjoyed baking, enjoyed helping somebody else, giving something for the church.

All through history it seemed there were always a lot of women active in the church, particularly over here. Now I don't know about the West Indies, but particularly over here you see more women than men in the church. Even in the Bible the Lord always referred to the women who were around: the disciples were doing the main work, but the women were always around. And even when there's social activity downstairs in the church there's only about three or four men — I don't know what's wrong with the men.

I did have that feeling within that the Lord wanted me to do something, and I had asked the Lord to show me whatever he wanted me to do. I decided I wanted to serve him. I was only about nine years old then. I remember I went to some special service with some other school children, and I decided I really wanted to step out with the Lord. I never seemed to have much worldly ambitions, never was attracted much to the worldly things. I was always more interested in things pertaining to the church, so I felt that the Lord had something particular for me to do. It's hard to explain just how you feel, but he shows it to you somehow.

I remember when I first came to Toronto, there was a friend of mine who was in another church and she used to have open air meetings. I remember a few times that she asked me to go with her it was down at the other church at Chestnut Street. There was quite a large space in the front where some people could stand around listening. Sometimes she'd ask me to give a testimony and I'd testify. And she said, "I think the Lord wants you to be a preacher, Addie," and I said, "No." I said, "I don't think I'll ever be a preacher." But it wasn't long after that that I felt the Lord was definitely speaking to me and telling me that he wanted me to go out and preach the Gospel. It's sort of hard to explain: you just have that feeling. Some say they hear the Lord's voice definitely, but it just seemed that within the Lord was showing me that that's what he wanted me to do: he wanted me to go out and preach. And so I was willing.

My parents weren't much in favour of me going into the church, particularly when I spoke of going out for missionary work. I wanted to go to Africa. After I started the Bible Club — 'cause there was several missionaries coming and talking — it seemed like for a while the need was so great.

Over here so many don't seem to appreciate the Gospel, but over there they respond so quick. Even in Halifax, they were so anxious because every church didn't have a minister there. Even now, every church doesn't have a minister because maybe they don't want to support one or something like that. But at least they have the opportunity of hearing the Gospel. But over in Africa they're somebody that don't hear the Gospel, and I felt that's what the Lord wanted me to do, I felt that's why he wanted me to go to Bible college. But the doors didn't seem to be open. I said, "Well, wherever the Lord opens the door, that's where I'll go."

I remember I spoke to one of the ministers, and I said at that time that I still wanted to go to Africa. And he said you could get Africa in Nova Scotia; he said, "There's a church here that needs you." And I said, "Well, maybe he sees me. Maybe there's a church. Maybe over there, there are people over there need me more. But I'm willing to go." Still, if there was no door open.... I tried different ways, but the door wasn't open. So I said, "Lord, wherever you want me to go." I'm very thankful that the Lord did put that desire in my heart while I was young.

It didn't seem to bother me much that I was a woman, except when the minister said he was going to put the resolution to the conference — then I begun to wonder what they were going to say and how am I going to react? After it was passed, I gave a word of thanks for my desires to do whatever was best. Before that I didn't have anything to say, but I was really wondering what would be their reaction and how I'd get along. And, of course, I was a little nervous for a while afterwards, but they received me very well.

Most of the men agreed. In fact, there was one woman that voted against me. She said, "We never had this, so I don't see why we have to have it now."

Maybe my strength isn't the same as years ago, but I still enjoy church work. I'm not tired of it. I'm not satisfied with just sitting around doing nothing, and when Sunday comes I feel that if I'm at all able I should be there. And then when I'm there I'm usually asked to do something. But now I'm the assistant general superintendent of the conference.

I had several opportunities to get married, but I just couldn't. It seemed they wanted me to give up the church work and I didn't want to do that — I didn't feel that was the Lord's will.

I remember when I was in North Buxton, and one of my neighbours went by, and he said he understood I was going to give up the church and marry this man in Chatham. I said, "Who told you that?" And he said, "Well, you buried his wife." I had to sit for his wife a few months before that. I said to myself: now I'll bury him too, and in about four or five months I did have service for him. I said to my neighbour that I wasn't interested because I wasn't giving up the church: I didn't feel I would be happy giving up the church, things wouldn't work out right, I wouldn't have the time to devote, and I wanted to devote all my time I had to the church work and the Lord.

There's only one woman candidate for the ministry now, a young woman in the Toronto church. She's on probation, studying for the ministry — we have a deaconess also, but that's just to assist. We've had two or three deaconesses, but they've just wanted to assist in the church where they were. This young woman was ordained, consecrated a deaconess last year at the conference. She says she doesn't feel like travelling. I said to her that when I was consecrated a deaconess I was supposed to travel, to serve as a deaconess to the conference, not just to the local church. I was to travel wherever the help was needed: if a minister wasn't well or was busy or something — wasn't able to do certain duties — I was supposed to go and help.

Right now, it's hard to say what the future is for the church. There doesn't seem to be many people coming in. I know all things are possible, but it's really not so encouraging right now. You get a few in and they're just in for a short time.

And we find that it's very, very difficult to encourage the young people to serve in the church because they have so many opportunities now. Most of them are looking at the finance and, of course, you can't blame them in a way. Even the women are employed; they're not home in the day, and on the weekend they're gone or busy. It's maybe not as essential now.

A lot of Black people keep drawn to the church. Now they have other things, but a few years ago that's all they had was the church: that's where they met for worship, and that's where they met for social activities, and that's all they could claim of their own.

Back then there was the Garvey movement. I read a few papers, met a few radicals, but I didn't attend their meetings, although I know that people where I stayed, they seemed quite interested. I know it was active, quite an active group for some years. But I didn't get to know too much about the intricacies, except I knew they were planning on going back to Africa — they were trying to get people to go back to Africa. I didn't get to know much of what was going on then, but my personal idea was that there were so many more opportunities over here. Why would they want to go back to Africa?

In those days when I first came to Toronto all the girls were working domestic. And then when the war came, there were some that were working at ammunition factories, and the men were working on the railroads or on the boats.

People weren't going out to demonstrations in those days; I don't know why. They seemed to be quite contented for a few years, and then, all of a sudden, they decided that they needed something different, but there weren't many demonstrations. There was a certain amount of prejudice. There was a certain amount in the schools and, in particular, in trying to get a job or if you wanted to rent a room. There wasn't so many renting rooms or a house — they had all kinds of excuses. I think it's progressed considerable, but still there's plenty of room for improvement.

I feel like there's nothing like following a calling. If you feel called for a particular type of work, give yourself to that because in the end you will not be happy or successful if you choose something else.

Isn't that funny that to me my life doesn't seem so

much, doesn't seem so unusual. As I say, I'm thankful to the Lord. He could have chose somebody else.

Notes

1. The Ontario town of Kitchener was founded in 1806 as Dutch Sand Hills. In 1830 it was renamed Berlin, but anti-German sentiments stirred by World War I led to it being renamed Kitchener in 1916.

2. Founded in Philadelphia in 1816, the African Methodist Episcopal Church was active in Upper Canada by the 1820s. As Addie Aylestock explains later, the British Methodist Episcopal Church split off from the African Methodist Episcopal in the mid-1850s, in part because of the urging of fugitive slaves who thought they would be safer from the reach of the U.S. Fugitive Slave Act if they were British subjects and protected by an all-Canadian organization. The first BME Church was established in Chatham in 1856.

3. For information on Africville's history and eventual demolition, see Winks, *op. cit.* and Dennis William Magill's *Africville: The Life and Death of a Canadian Black Community* (Toronto, McClelland and Stewart, 1974).

Bertha McAleer

1909

I was born in Amherstburg, Ontario, 1909. Amherstburg is right across from Windsor. I just stayed there two years. The reason that we were there at the time was my father was a minister and he was a presiding elder over many churches that we had. We had a church at Hamilton at that time and all these different churches — in fact, there was a church in Winnipeg at one time — and my father worked in and around these churches for a long time.

The BME Church came out of the AME Church. That was about 1850 something when the split came in the churches. And the reason that it did was on account of slavery: they felt that if it was all British, that people coming over would have a better chance, so that's why we went out with the British for a while — the British Methodist — with the idea that when the slavery was over we would all go back to the AME, but they didn't. There's not so many coloured churches in Canada as such.

My grandmother, my mother's mother, came from Dublin, Ireland. She came to Chatham, and she married a Mr. Smith who came over from the States, so my mother's maiden name was Smith. Her family had three boys and she lived the longest, right there in Chatham. She was left here with the home at Chatham.

My father was born in Mount Vernon, Ohio, so when I was small his parents were the only grandparents that I didn't really know. His mother was alive in Mount Vernon — I remember she died when I was very small — but I'd never seen her. My father came over from the States and took charge of the church in Chatham and married my mother. They were right there and coming to church, so they met.

I had two brothers and one sister — one brother is still alive and last July I lost one of my brothers. My sister and my eldest brother — he's alive now — were born in Chatham, and then they moved on to Hamilton. My youngest brother was born in Hamilton, then we were asked to Amherstburg — and I was born in Amherstburg, then on to Toronto.

My brother that died last July, he was born in Hamilton and he used to be a long distance runner — Grant Abraham Hackley — he took part in that Boston Marathon. He also had a scout troop — the only coloured scout troop that I know of — within the church. That was quite a few years ago and a lot of the young men are still alive that were in that. It was a long time ago.

I come to Toronto at maybe 1911. My father was a pastor of the church in Toronto. When we first came to Toronto we were living just off of Front Street — Draper, that's where the parsonage was. When we first came here we weren't on University Avenue, they were worshipping in a hall. But after 1911, they moved to University Avenue, where the Sick Children's Hospital is now. We stayed there on University Avenue until 1929, and then the church moved from there to Soho Street, where we are now. My father died in '29, and when he died he was presiding elder over what they call the Northwestern Conference — that was around Minneapolis. We have churches all over the world.

Naturally, being the minister's wife, my mother was working in the missionary work. In fact, she started back in Chatham before I was born. She was one of the ones that started the missionary work in the African Methodist Episcopal Church — the one here in Toronto is called the Grant African Methodist Church, named after the Bishop Grant.

The thing of it is, years ago the first missionary work really started with ministers and with the men. But when I say missionary work, in that day and time when my mother is coming along — people didn't have that much. If someone would have a baby or something, the government wasn't giving you as much as what they're doing now today, so in the church we'd make different things for the children. Then, of course, there's always the foreign work: the church raises money to help the people in foreign countries.

My mother was a widow from 1929. She died in 1960 in her 88th year. She was a wonderful person and she always treated us the same: if there was anything to be divided any time, we would all have an equal share. She was always very strict in your morals and upbringing.

There's an awful lot of work that she used to do: families needed things, and you really looked after people then because you didn't have so much; you were always taking them baskets of food and things like this, and she was always attending the conference. I think with most churches, what would they do without the women?! Really!

My father was sent out to Iowa and we were there two years. I being still in school, I had to go with my mother.

My two brothers and sisters had positions here in Toronto, so they could stay here.

I was seventeen, eighteen years old, and then I was still in school, 'cause when I come back I went to the high school, Eastern High School of Commerce, and when I finished there I took up hairdressing, with Mme. Brewton. I was there at the Brewtons quite a few years with her. She was a person that was very outgoing.

I worked with her and I was able to use my work; she sent out letters to her customers and I would type out letters. And, in the meantime, I also went to night school, Central Tech, and I took sewing and cooking; then I took a public speaking course at the Central, so that helped me a lot in my church work because at times you're given a job to speak, and you had to introduce somebody.

I do remember in the Depression I was working for Mme. Brewton and she had a Jewish clientele — lots of them had invested in stocks, lost everything — came in there crying. It was a terrible time, it was a terrible time. And back then too, I can remember my girlfriend — I've known her since then and we're still in contact with one another — and her father got out of work. Back there you weren't just getting unemployment like you're getting now, and she had to look after the family. She had two other sisters. She kept them going for a long time till the father got a job. So back there in the 1930s it wasn't easy; it was hard and it must've been for everybody. Particular family that I'm speaking about, they were white. It was hard; it was hard, very hard.

The Brewtons rented this hall and along with that they had public speaking contest. There was about eight of us took part in the public speaking contest. Margaret and I — she was the minister's daughter at the BME Church — we were kind of left in the contest. The subject was about abolishing the corporal punishment in the public schools in Toronto. So I just won out, I humbly say, over Margaret, and I got the diamond ring. But this was a wonderful thing, and this was put on by Dr. and Mme. Brewton, and they used their money to help different things and their church as well. They're First Baptist Church.

Then also we formed a tennis club, Ramsden Park, up on Yonge Street, play tennis — and that was sort of in with her group too. And we had what you call the Flower Circle — we had someone come in and teach us Jamaican flowers and arrangements and we made a lot of these.

When it come to Mother's Day a couple of us would stand outside the Baptist Church — in those days, people thought more about Mother's Day in a way — they must wear their roses — and so we made these white roses and red roses and we would sell them. It would all help the church.

In that day and time, of course, people weren't earning a lot of money, so I think that people lived a little simpler lives; we didn't have all this stuff. There was always something going on because you really didn't have your TV. You weren't interested in sitting home and looking at TV like the people are today, and we had more community things. We went to church, and the young people were doing more plays, more social things than what you have today. They do have things today, but it's hard to get the average person interested in that because they have their own things to do.

I think the church played maybe a greater role then because people were, generally speaking, more church-minded. There wasn't so many things to take them away from it as there is today, but I still think that sometimes a few can be powerful — doesn't always take a great mob. A few can be powerful and there is a few that are hanging in there.

There wasn't a lot of coloured people in the place — it's not like coming here today. I went to Earl Grey School on Strathcona Avenue, and if I remember one other that would have to be about it besides myself. I would go downtown and walk around, and I would nearly always run into somebody I know because there wasn't that many. And then, of course, at that time it was very hard for girls to get into hospitals as nurses — you may have the odd one and you have the odd one in stores — but you wouldn't see them like you do today.

But then people kind of thought more of one another. We as a group of coloured people in Toronto were closer together because a lot of the people lived downtown — we always lived more or less out, but we were going all the time 'cause my father was a minister. The people lived more central: there was Sullivan Street and Dundas, and all around there was a lot of coloured people that were living there. The odd one — maybe a few — would have their own homes, but they were renting down around there, and it made a difference.

Now these days the odd person you can look at and get a smile out of them, but some of the them you better not: they look as if they just don't want to be bothered with you. That sort of a friendliness, a closeness — it's kind of gone except with some people.

I think things are better for our people 'cause I see them getting different jobs — government and Eaton's store and all the stores, and nursing — they're getting into all these places. I'm happy for that, but as for the group in here as I have known it, we are further apart because we are just all over this place now. But generally speaking, I think it's good.

The best place of any country of this world to live? Canada is the best. I believe it is the best, although things have changed; we have more crime than we used to have, but not really compared to other places. Now, you would expect to have a little more because you have a lot more people, so I think you have to be a little careful where you go and who you're mingling with because if you get in there — in with the wrong crowd — you're going to get into trouble.

I think it's marvellous what the women are into. They're into about everything. They have more advantages and more opportunities — my! I love to see them in broadcasting and the TV and this sort of thing. Women can play a big role because of that. I think they have the patience and all, they can exceed. When they really get in there at the job, they do a good job, they work hard.

After I married, until my son was born, I was doing some work on my own, and when the war came on I was doing war work out there. They had a place set up out in Scarborough. There wasn't too many coloured people working there from what I can remember, but there was some.

I guess if I was thinking about it today, maybe I wouldn't have done that with the way you feel about war. But at that time it was good money; we were really filling these shells, when I come to think of it — my goodness, the place could've blown up! You didn't really think too much about it, not when you're younger. When you went in you took a shower; when you went out you took a shower, in case the powder gets on you — and I never did like showers. I always liked baths.

I don't think the war years was very much different from the way the people'd been feeling, even in other races, all along. I think young men are just eager; I don't think they're thinking about what might happen. Personally, I don't like to think of war because you're just wondering if they'll ever come back. Even now, especially in the States, young men are going for different things, and they're not expecting things to happen, but they're killing people. But the war gave a lot of different work to women. I think maybe that was the part: the women kind of started doing work.

Then later on, when my children became teenagers, I took a job in Don Mills. We were sorting the mail and doing changes of addresses, and sometimes if they got busy we'd work full-time. Otherwise we would come in the month when they sort all these cheques — the old age, all these different things. We worked for about ten years, then they brought in computers, and when they brought in computers it was transferred down to the main post office, and we were let go. But I did love that job.

And another thing, you always said "coloured people" because at that time "Black" was a fighting word and I don't know why it should've been. It really was and even today I cannot say it. I can't. It was used in a negative way; that's what it was.

You know today you think of it in a different light altogether. I was out to see my daughter one day, walking along the street, and for some reason or other I had to go in and see a coloured family, and I had forgotten where the coloured family lived. So I seen a little boy come along, and I said to the little boy, "You know where the coloured family is?" He said to me, "What colour?" I thought: Isn't this strange? And it just dawned on me: I guess he's not used to that. I said, "Brown," and he said, "Oh yes, they live right down there."

That's one thing that I'm happy about: that people have come and you're not looking at somebody because their colour; you don't know who is coloured anyways to tell you the truth! Because you go over to the Toronto islands — I remember I went over to a picnic and I said to myself: now I'm going to look for my group, a coloured group. I went over and it wasn't my group at all! There is so many groups and so many people from different countries that the colour of the skin doesn't mean anything anymore. Because you could come from India — you could even be from Japan or anything.

My husband he worked at People's Jewellers — it was People's Credit Jewellers then. First, he was a shipping clerk, and then he let them know that he could be something different, something very artistic. He said to Mr. Guerstein, who died, "You give me a chance and I will show you what I can do." The boss made him head of the display department; they built all of those the stands for the rings — all the stands — and they would do this for all of the stores — three months or so before Christmas they would get all this work done. He give him a chance to see what he could do, and my husband worked there for forty years.

Most all of the stuff here in my house he made. He's quite artistic and my son he's the same way. He took a course four years at the art college.

I have seen such a change in life that I can hardly believe it. You didn't have so many highrises in Toronto back then. My goodness, it has an awful lot of highrises. You go out places and they're so drastically changed you hardly recognize. Like the Old City Hall — I'm so glad that wasn't torn down because it's a lovely building. But there was drastic changes around the city, places you hardly know — an awful lot. In fact, I think it's been developed too fast; it's costly.

I feel sorry for people who have to go and find a place to live. Everybody is flocking here because of the work. It's too expensive unless you've got your home paid for already. I have my home paid for years ago, and now you could get around 200,000 dollars where you paid maybe 15,000. I can understand that things would go up, but 200,000 is far beyond what it should be. Then if you buying a home it will take two to be working. You can probably go to a smaller place and get accommodation a little cheaper, but there's no work, and they'll have to commute into Toronto. And because so many people are working — they have to be these days because the cost of everything — I think a lot of the way that food is prepared is killing people: they're not eating a simple thing; everything is fixed up.

In that day and time, of course, it was different: the majority of women were not working; the mothers were not working. But I think it is wonderful in these days when I see these mothers. I look at my own daughter — she's got three! — and she's managing wonderful and trying to train them children to do things and keep busy, and it's hard.

I've never belonged to any other church but the AME, so today I'm still working in the church: I sing in the choir — not that I have such a beautiful voice, but I just enjoy it.

I am a class leader — in our church the members are divided up into classes — and I have a certain number in my class that I look after: they're not out for some day, I'm checking on them; perhaps they're sick or something, or they need something, so then I let the pastor know and he goes to visit them. Whatever is needed. You just keep in contact; you have an idea about the life of the person, and you try to help them. So many things happen: children to be baptised; things are coming up in your life; you have a problem and you're looking to somebody. Sometimes a friend wants to help you, but they don't have maybe all the answers, so I think the church there is a wonderful thing. Sometimes you see a different light on it, or you listen to a problem or something, and then you go to another church, but you have a driving faith. You keep smiling — some people think they have to be so sanctimonious, but it's not so — you still enjoy life in the right way.

The night comes, the day comes, and we don't have one thing to do with it! But God does. That's the way I think. It isn't as if you have to be going to church all the time. But you must have that way of life to keep you going.

Viola Berry Aylestock
1910

I was born in 1910, February the fourteenth. Momma's little valentine.

My mother, Mary Elizabeth Mott, was born in Toronto, and my father, William James, was born in Hamilton. My father's mother was born just outside of Hamilton; when she was a child in the 1800s she used to open and close the toll gate at the top of James Street, which at that time was called the Hamilton Mountain. The farmers used to bring their wares down to the Hamilton market, and she would open and close the toll gate and take their money.

My father's father, Henry Berry, was an escaped slave; he came up through the Underground Railway through the St. Catharines area.

My mother's mother, Mary Thomas, was born in Montreal and her background was most unusual: her mother, my great-grandmother, had been found on an island off the coast of Java by two Scotsmen; by the mark on her forehead they knew that she had belonged to a royal family.

She was the only one left on the island — a typhoon had hit the island — so they picked her up, took her in a boat back to Scotland. She was put in a boarding school and she was educated there. I had three great-aunts and two great-uncles who were born in Edinburgh, near the University of Edinburgh.

When she became older she met my great-grandfather. He had come to Edinburgh with the family that he was working with — he was a butler — so the two of them became married, then her husband was brought back to Canada with these people — this is how she came back with her family. My grandmother was one of the ones born in Montreal.

Her first husband, my mother's father, was one of the first Black barbers here in Toronto; he had a shop right across the road from where Osgoode Hall is now on Queen Street — this would be in the late 1800s. I really don't know where she met him; all I know about my mother's father is that he had come from Niagara Falls. Now whether his people had come up through that area from the south, I don't know.

All I remember is her speaking about her husband and how he died very suddenly: he went fishing one day and he was dead in two days; a catfish bone got in his hand and the poison went through his system. At that time there weren't any antibiotics like there is today, so he died and left a young married woman with three small children.

She had to provide for these children, but the only technique that she really had to make a living with was sewing, so she used to sew overalls for factories in Toronto, and this is how she raised her family. At that time most women brought their work home because it was necessary so you could watch your children. It was a real struggle; in fact, more so I feel for my grandmother — she had never worked in her life hard.

She had the most beautiful hands I had ever seen. She never went to a public school; she had been educated in a French convent in Montreal — that's where she learned to sew and to tat and to knit. She taught me to knit when I was five, which I did very well, but I never could catch onto the tatting — it was so intricate. She talked to me in French as a little girl, which I promptly forgot.

When her husband died — he had bought property out in the east end of Toronto, but with her being a woman, in those days you knew nothing, absolutely nothing about your husband's business — so consequently, she didn't receive any of her husband's property.

My grandmother married for a second time after her first husband died. Her second husband was a bricklayer and he worked on the Old City Hall when that was being constructed.[1] After that they moved to Hamilton and he had a job in the Hamilton Steel Company.

My mother, I imagine, met my father at church — at that time that's where you were supposed to meet eligible young men. So they married; then the First World War came, and my father enlisted, and we were still living with my grandmother.

After the war, my father had a bad cough — he had a job in a factory as a buffer. When he went back for a check-up, they thought that he had TB, so he spent a year in the Hamilton sanatorium. But it wasn't TB that he had, it was just a heavy bronchial cough from sleeping in the trenches in France during the war. When he came out of the san, he decided at that time, like so many men did, that he would become a porter, so he came down to Toronto and got on the CPR.[2] That was the early twenties — 1924, I think it was — and from then on we lived in Toronto. At that time we lived in the east end; now it's called the centre of the city, but when we moved to Rhodes Avenue, everybody used to say, "Why do you live way out in the country?"

My mother never worked; she was always at home and took care of the house because my grandmother was a great churchwoman. Most of the time she was gone so many days a week with another lady; they rented a carriage, and they went around soliciting funds for the church, so my mother was the one that stayed at home.

I had one brother; we were a very close family. All our friends were Black. Our home was the house where young people continually gathered after church or birthday parties, after tennis. My sister and I played tennis, had a lot of fun, but after tennis the gang came out to our house. My mother always had plenty of refreshments; we had the piano and a couple of the chaps could play the piano. We just had something. My mother had never worked in her life outside of the home, so this was what her life centred around: the home.

We had my grandmother living with us, my mother's mother. She had been an invalid for eighteen years — the last ten years was terrible because she developed cancer, and the cancer was on the outside of the breast, so consequently she went in, and she had that breast removed. She came home, she took a stroke — and in those days you just didn't have any help at all; you might have a visiting nurse, if you asked for it, but that's about all the help that you got. And nobody, nobody went to a nursing home. My grandmother really took over the whole house: everything centred around my grandmother and my mother was worked out of her feet.

With my grandmother being an invalid like that, it really took the toll on the whole place. After she had the cancer operation — she was one of the first people to receive radium for the treatment of cancer after an operation — they gave her too strong of a dose and it affected her mind. It was quite a time, and this went on for eighteen years, with the washing to be done and the changing of the bed and all.

Now that I look back, I realize just how clever my mother was. This is the way it is with most mothers, but we don't realize it at the time. I can remember her always saying that you must get an education, but don't become an educated fool. In other words, don't be a bore with it. My mother was a woman with foresight. She always said that it never hurt to carry an education: you could carry it without any stress or strain, and the more knowledge you had, the easier it was for you to make a good living. She just figured that if we get an education, things were bound to open up, which they did.

The first day I started school — looking back now — it was tragic. When I left kindergarten and went in grade one, I had a teacher — I can see her now, Mrs. Brown, she wore a brown outfit — and she was so strict that I really believe it had a psychological effect on me. Thinking back, I feel that her attitude had a very, very bad effect on me. I honestly can't say that colour had anything to do with it; she was just strict.

There weren't any other Blacks there at that school — this was the first school I went to in Hamilton. Then we came down to Toronto, and, being a larger city, there was more Blacks. That would be around 1925.

It was a large school in Toronto, Ogden Public School, downtown, and in that area it was mostly Jewish. There was maybe a handful of Blacks. I was interested in the easy subjects: geography, spelling and history. I certainly wasn't mathematically inclined — in fact, I had a fear of mathematics; a blockage, this is what I had where math was concerned.

My first job was working for a shoemaker. He had a store way out on the Danforth, and I would go there three days a week and take in the shoes there; he and his wife went out and did something else — I don't know what they did — so I was a clerk there.

After that, I got a job as a maid in one of the biggest hairdressing parlours in Canada at that time; there was fifty hair cubicles there. I also did all their mail, so this is why I know that their toupees and wigs and face preparations and everything were mailed all over Canada.

I worked there five years. While I was there I went to night school three nights a week at Jarvis Collegiate. I had been at Jarvis for a year, so I went back at night; I wanted to get my matriculation. I also went for a while to Harbord Collegiate. This was around 1929. I never finished — the Depression hit.

The Depression hit, so I got a job as a general help. Sometimes they lasted and sometimes they didn't; sometimes I lived in and sometimes I didn't. I can't remember how many different families I worked for in a year; it was quite a few. You really worked hard. When you lived in you had your room at night — thank God I liked to read — but you're so tired that you just fell into bed at night anyway, and there weren't any TVs in those days.

If you lived in, you were lucky to make thirty dollars a month; you started at seven in the morning and you still weren't through at seven in the evening — it depended on the size of the family. One job I had, I stayed not quite the month. She took the thirty dollars and she divided the days into thirty dollars so that I wouldn't get my full pay. There was nine people in that family. I can remember cooking a fifteen pound roast and putting it on a silver tray to bring into the dining room — the dining room was over sixteen feet long — carrying this heavy roast up to the man of the house. It was very wealthy homes that I was in. The treatment was not the greatest, and I did that for ten years.

I married Archie Thompson at twenty-three and we moved. My husband was from Barrie, so naturally I went to Barrie. Archie came from a large family; his father at one time had been a farmer, and they were from the area around Oro, where the Black church is now situated; his father came from there and his mother too.

His father left the farm, came into Barrie, and he got a job at the CNR run house;[3] it was a good paying job, so they stayed there. Must've had about five girls, four boys.

When I married my husband the father and mother were dead, so there was just a sister living and the brother living in the homestead. My husband used to come down to Toronto periodically — there was very few Blacks in Barrie, so the young Thompson family used to come down to Toronto quite often — and this is how I met him.

It was quite a traumatic experience for somebody who had lived in the city. Barrie was very small and it was made up of retired farmers. The war had just started, so there were people there from all over living in rented rooms and anything they could get to live in.

I stayed at home, but being a small town, you soon got to know the neighbour across the road and the neighbour next door. Every morning we'd have our coffee at one of their houses, and we'd be there till quarter to twelve — when we saw our husbands come up the street to come home for lunch, we'd make a dash. So it was a pretty good life for a while. I didn't have any children. At that time my husband had a good job; he was a supervisor in a tanning factory.

Barrie was a town of retired farmers, so there wasn't much industry there. I can remember we had a family, a white family, living upstairs in our home; they had come down from Gravenhurst — there wasn't a thing in Gravenhurst, so they came to Barrie and both him and her got a job in the tanning factory where my husband was. So they started to build, but they stayed with us for the winter because the house wasn't finished. And she worked. She had to work. I can remember her now going down the steps in twenty below zero weather, six-thirty in the morning; she worked for twenty cents an hour in a meat-packing plant.

For a while I worked at the tannery. There were a lot of women hired — women had been there for years — and they dyed the skins as they came on the belt. And, of course, I wanted something to do and I wanted more money. So finally with the war on they really needed women: they needed help because the men just weren't there, so finally I got a job there, in the early '40s, over my husband's objections.

The war was over and things had opened up for the Blacks — again you find the influx of the people from the islands. I find it wasn't them coming that had an influence on things opening up. I think the whole thing opened up with the war: more was demanded and consequently they had to have more people in jobs; this was the turning point for Blacks.

Before that there just wasn't any jobs — the odd job there was; people wrote their civil service job (exam) and they were accepted. But even at that time before the war white people were still unemployed — hundreds and hundreds of white people too. And now that I look back on it, a white person couldn't even get a job in a bank unless they knew somebody, so you can't say that we were the only ones that were unemployed because we weren't.

Then the unions started to come to Barrie and get into these places, so the wages went up gradually. I was in the union for a while when my husband worked at the plant in Barrie. I got to thinking: this is ridiculous the money you're making here — I forget how much it was an hour. So when the union came to town and I heard about it — they came to the factory after hours — I joined.

My father was always a union person. My father was a porter on the road. I can remember he was a real CCF man; I know he really believed in the CCF — a lot of the army men who had been to both wars were CCF.[4] He always voted CCF and he always told everybody else to vote CCF.

We were connected with the fur workers — I forget their real title — but we came under them because of the skins. My husband lost his job as supervisor because he was all in favour: he was telling all his men to make sure they signed up for the union and vote for the union and, of course, that got back to management and he lost his job.

The union came up from Toronto, and back then we had the meetings down at the Royal York — I had to come down for meetings and the conventions and I'd go back up to Barrie.

I got to be secretary of the local for about two years and I really solicited for higher wages, better hours, all this stuff. There were a few other women that had signed up in the union, but on the executive it was strictly men, and myself as secretary; there may have been other Blacks in the union in Toronto because we were connected with the fur and leather workers in Toronto — so there may have been Black men in the union — but if I remember rightly, it was strictly a Jewish union.

As secretary I attended all the meetings and I made notation of everything that took place. When we had conventions I came down to Toronto and attended the conventions and took reports back. But we didn't last too long because the company closed for a while and we were squeezed out. The union stopped because the factory closed down — they were so opposed to a union in Barrie, my heavens! This plant had been a one-family affair for years — it went way, way back — and they were appalled to think that somebody would try to get a union in their plant, so it closed down, and we all lost our jobs, my husband included. He was supervisor, but he had gone behind management's back and told everybody to join the union.

My husband got another job as the desk man at a hotel — nights, twelve o'clock midnight — and then he got a better job at Camp Borden. It was a good job, outfitting the men in the army. That was a steady job and, of course, with his athletic ability — he had been a boxer — he soon became involved with the army. Although he was a civilian, he was really highly rated and he trained boxers out there. Also, having been in baseball — he had been an umpire in baseball for years, he was connected with the Ontario Athletic Association — he had ball teams out there for the soldiers and he made quite a name for himself.

Friends of mine were in the military. The husband is from Nova Scotia and his sister came up and joined the army. She wanted to become a nurse, so she joined the army, and in three years' time she had her RN, and she was a very good nurse too. This was in the late 1950s.

She graduated and then she was posted to different

places: she was up in White Horse, then Churchill. In fact, I think it was in Churchill that she met her husband. There were very few soldiers up there at that time and, of course, not many Blacks, but she met him there. He was a sergeant. She got out of the army and settled with him in Toronto. Then it was time for him to be pensioned off, so they have a very good living through the army.

I have heard of other Black girls being in the army, but I haven't heard of any Black person being in the air force — for an education, for a cheap education you just can't beat the army. I know there's discipline and everything, but there should be discipline in all walks of life, not only the army and not only the forces.

My husband was forty-nine when he died, shovelling snow, but he had had a heart condition for a while, which we didn't realize. It was quite a shock. I stayed in Barrie, must've been two years after that. The year after he died, I was still in the house, but I had rented part of it out to friends. After they were transferred — he was in the army — I decided to sell the house, so I sold, and my aunt came up from Toronto, and we got an apartment. I got a job in the Barrie hospital — old Victoria Hospital — and it was through working there that I became interested in food.

I put an application in Toronto here with the Ontario Hospital Association to take a course as a food supervisor, so my aunt kept the apartment for the year, and she kept her job at the air force at Camp Borden — she was a cook. I came down here and stayed with a friend and took the course.

I graduated in '64. That was another traumatic experience: I ended up with a terrible ulcer from studying; after years and years of being out of school, you go back and you have these young teachers. It's tough. When I graduated I got a job in Toronto General as a food supervisor. I was there over two years, and then I decided I'd like another job because of the money — hospitals never did pay much.

It was a good move — I got a job with the government as a correctional officer. I wrote an exam for that job: it was an all-day exam from nine to twelve, and from one to four, and it was quite tough. We even had questions where a — let's say psychotherapist — had a stop watch on us. We had so many minutes for each page of questions. Out of the two hundred that wrote, I think there were ten of us that were hired. Two other Blacks had already passed this exam; one was a registered nurse originally from Guyana, but she had received her nurse's training in England; the other gal was from Guyana too.

It was a good move for me 'cause not only was the salary better, but I felt that I had been started on a new career — a career where I felt that I could help young girls who had been into trouble with the law, so I stayed there.

First I worked at the old Mercer on Queen Street — that's where I really was initiated. After a time the government closed up Mercer — they had been in the meantime building a new place for girls out in Brampton called the Vanier Centre for Women.[5]

It was built on a new plan, a plan that originated, if I'm not mistaken, in California, and if you were to see the set up, you would think it was a women's college. And, of course, all the girls were clothed and the educational system was terrific: they went to school every day, and those that wanted to take hairdressing went to the hairdressing school, so it really had its advantages. As I told girls when they came up for parole, if they couldn't make it on the outside now, it was nobody's fault but their own.

There were very few Blacks in the institution. Once in a while we would get the odd woman from the States. I can remember two in particular that had come over from Chicago: they had taken fur coats from Eaton's and they were preparing to wear them back across the line; one had made a slip up — she kept the ticket from the coat in her wallet — and this is how they caught her. Two lovely women. They were there nine months — but really nice people, easy to get along with them — and their lawyers finally got them out.

You learned so much about human nature. Some would break down and tell their experiences, their childhood, how they came up. So many of the girls were from broken homes. I had one young girl tell me how her father had molested her for years and her sister also. I worked at Vanier from 1964 to 1973. With the changing of shifts all the time my health broke, so the doctor suggested I take another job; but I decided I had worked long enough, so I took an early retirement.

It was hard being a Black person: the fact that you had the education and you still couldn't get the jobs really that you were fitted for — it was frustrating and that's why so many Blacks left. I can remember my mother saying that in the early 1900s some friends of our family left, and they went and settled in Cincinnati. They found, just like so many people do, that the streets aren't paved with gold, no matter where you go. They made big money in the States, but they worked hard for big money, and so many of them became ill, like their systems couldn't take it. They bought property and everything, but they never lived to enjoy the property, so who wins in the end?

When my husband and I were coming up, we knew that we were Black, but it was never emphasized. When this

Black thing took over, I'm telling you, we older people, we laughed — so what? We know we're Black ... emphasize it so? But, of cours[e] ... ty. I can remember a friend ... they had to have the Afro h[air] ... ma, you just don't understa[nd] ... ell, I do understand! I've be[en] ... [w]ouldn't I understand?" Oh L[ord] ... utiful — well Brown is Beaut[iful] ...

I've been a mem[ber of the Eureka] Club for near ten years. I'm one of the younger ones in service as far as the Eureka goes; gradually our members are dwindling, which can be expected, but we go way back in history. We're in our seventy-seventh year. Research has been done, and it has been found that we are the oldest women's club in Canada that has stayed together over the years. Mary Ball was one of the founding members. At one time the Black women — senior women in Montreal had a club — but from what I can find out, it has finally given up.

Most of the women in the Eureka now are in their seventies and eighties. I'm one of the youngest. Bee Allen is younger; she's seventy-five. Verda Cook, she's seventy.

We don't have the social obligations in the Eureka that we used to have because the government has taken over. At one time, years and years ago, we used to supply baskets of food and see that a person's rent was paid and this sort of thing. We don't have to worry about that any more: if you haven't any money for your rent, then you just go to a government agency or the Salvation Army. The only thing we can really do now is visit the sick and keep in touch by sending them cards, and we donate funds towards scholarships.

It must be remembered that, as we get older, we do pass

away, and this is what is happening, and we aren't getting any newer, younger members. I wish the daughters of the younger members would come in and take over — then we could be members emeritus — so we must look into this and see if they would take over.

Notes

1. The City of Toronto's Old City Hall opened September 18, 1899.

2. The Canadian Pacific Railway.

3. The Canadian National Railway.

4. The forerunner of the NDP (the New Democratic Party), the Cooperative Commonwealth Federation, founded in 1932 in Alberta, drew its members from farmers and labour organizations, Christians involved in the social gospel movement and socialists.

5. The Vanier Centre for Women.

Bee Allen

1911

I was born in 1911, October the fourteenth.

My father is from the United States and came from Ohio — the name of the place is just gone from me for the moment. My mother, Edna Parker, was born in Canada, and her mother was born in Pennsylvania, U.S.A.; her mother was a white Dutch lady, by the name of Baldwin. My mother's father was Richard Ball, and he was born in St. Catharines, Ontario, of a man named Henry Ball who came from the States with his father; the father came over here with his two sons and made their home here, and Richard Ball married Mary Jackson.

Used to be a paper here called *The Evening Telegram*. This is what it says about my grandfather:

> Mr. Ball had been pastor of a church in Toronto. He was born in St. Catharines in 1845, son of the Reverend Henry Ball, who had formerly been a slave on a plantation in Virginia. The father escaped to the north in the company with his brother and settled in St. Catharines where he frequently preached. He died

when Richard was eight years old and the boy grew up in St. Catharines.[1]

His father's home was one of the stations of the Underground Railway by which many slaves escaped from the South. Both Reverend Mr. Ball and his brother assisted many slaves to escape into Canada; in many instances as a boy he met the escaped slaves at Niagara and gathered them in safety to St. Catharines.[2]

My grandfather died and was buried in Toronto on December 29, 1925; this was reported and his picture was in the paper.

My grandmother and grandfather travelled with the family; they were known as the Ball Family Jubilee Singers, and they travelled from coast to coast. I have a picture of the whole Ball family. Besides my grandmother and grandfather, there were two sons and two daughters, including my mother: that was the Ball Family Jubilee Singers. They sang some spiritual music, also some Southern type of music, slave music. *The Evening Telegram* says: "Their public career as evangelistic singers began in Grimsby, Ontario, when in 1877 the late Reverend Dr. Hugh Johnson invited them to sing. Mr. Ball was also invited to sing in Toronto many years ago, first by F.S. Spence." I know that's so because I was in later years out at some affair, and I met the daughter of this F.S. Spence, and she had a copy of this picture on her mantle she told me.

A lot of what I knew was because my mother talked to me about it and I was around my grandmother in her later years. If they wanted to sing they took my mother — and my grandfather often spoke in public — and many times my grandmother was accompanied, of course, by my mother. My grandmother sang; and many times, she would speak in the evening at different churches or public places, so my grandmother would be the soloist, and my mother would play for my grandfather and my grandmother to sing duets. They would take along myself, as a child, and a cousin to sing with them.

I know for one thing mother said my grandfather talked about the days of slavery and many of the things that happened. He talked from what he heard from his father and his mother.

Now this talk about travelling across Canada — when they were small they would travel by train, and mother has often talked about the things that she remembered of the travelling.

My grandmother and grandfather had ten children, eight of which they raised. My mother said lots of times, they were left with their Grandmother Hussey — she was English — in St. Catharines when Grandpa and Grandma would be away.

My grandfather, he joined the BME conference, and he pastored in London and Toronto. My mother was in a situation where she had family, but my father had defected, I'll say. She stayed around with my grandmother and grandfather, so I was raised really closer to my grandmother and grandfather.

My grandmother was the type of person that she relied on my mother to help her because my grandmother was one of the few coloured ministers who went where her husband went: she was not being left behind; if my grandfather was sent some place to pastor, my grandmother went. She didn't stay back as some of them did and say, "Well, I'm not taking the children out of school." She went, and when they got older and certain things came up, if my grandmother needed someone to represent her, she sent my mother.

When they decided to send my grandfather to Winnipeg, Manitoba to open the BME Church there, naturally my grandmother was going with him. At that particular time, my aunt was ill — she had married and moved to Cleveland, Ohio — and my mother, with my brother and I, had been sent by my grandmother to help in my aunt's home, to stay there and nurse her because my grandmother couldn't do it, and she felt she should, but she was going with her husband wherever he was.

Now when this aunt died, her husband asked if we two children and my mother could stay, and he felt why shouldn't we stay there? My grandmother said no: she didn't see that my mother could stay there in that home; she's not married to her brother-in-law. I would presume that it was desecration to even think that my mother could. My grandmother ruled that out.

Now my grandfather had been sent to Winnipeg, so my grandmother bundled us up, my mother and my brother and I, and up to Winnipeg we went. My grandfather was prominent there, as the only other Black minister who was in Winnipeg, and he had opened a Black church.

He was also quite a good speaker. My grandmother did have a very nice voice and she sang. My mother was a proficient accompanyist and she played for my grandmother. So, many times my grandfather'd be asked to speak, and he would take my grandmother along, and my grandmother would take my mother, and my mother would go and take my brother and I. We were taught to sing spirituals along with them, so that would be the evening that my grandfather would provide.

Later the BME conference decided that my grandfather

was an older man and maybe they would send a younger man up there to carry on the work. The AME Church had gone up there too, and the AME minister and my grandfather worked very closely, as my grandfather was that type of person. At that time, the AME minister was a Mr. Hackley and the two men — my grandfather and Mr. Hackley — just worked it together. They took the attitude "Just come to church. If you want to be AME now, ok. If you want to be BME now, ok." And that's how they settled it. But they decided to move my grandfather down to Toronto; they were going to give him the Toronto charge and so they brought him down from Winnipeg. We went to Winnipeg in 1919 and we came back in '21.

He came down and the parsonage was already occupied by the minister that was in charge at the time. They were going to move him elsewhere. But, in the meantime, we lived at this aunt's house and this aunt died. Then my grandmother and grandfather moved to the parsonage and took my uncle and the three children and my mother and we two into the parsonage.

I was the one that remembers most of the things. I only wished that I had been a little older; if I had been a little older, I perhaps would have seen the necessity of writing down some of the things, but instead of that I was just around all the time, hearing the church talk and things that were going on and family talk and everything. Of all the family, I'm the one to tell them things of what went on because I'm the one that was there and I listened.

I was concerned when we moved. I was always the one to ask, "Oh, what are we going to do there?" And I was always the one that my mother explained what we were supposed to do because I always lived in somebody else's home. I had a very strong sense of "in your home we do what you want." My consolation was that when I have my own home I'll do what I want, but I respect very strongly your right to do what you want in your own home because I was always taught: you're in your grandmother's home, you're in your Aunt Winnie's home, you're in your Aunt Sophie's home.

It doesn't mean that I didn't feel loved and I didn't feel welcome; I have to say I felt welcome in those homes, but this was my mother's approach to it. They never had to be cross with me or critical of me because my mother made sure that I respected their rights.

I did not as a child notice difficulties, but, in retrospect, yes, it was difficult as a woman. There were struggles that my mother faced: there were struggles that she faced that white women did not have.

My mother never had a home of her own and she always respected the rights of others. When I was in the same Eureka Club as my mother I used to say to her, "When you're going to take your turn entertaining the Eurekas, why don't you say, 'Come to my home this next time'? You always say, 'Come to my daughter's home.' You always invite them to your daughter's home, and when they get up to thank you for your hospitality" — which they always did — "you always said, 'Thank you for thanking me. I will see that my daughter is aware of your appreciation because it is through her that I'm entertaining today.' " And I said, "But that isn't necessary." That's how I felt.

She said, "It is necessary; it's your home." She said, "I never knew what it was to have a home, but I'm so happy that you do that I want you to have all the things that go with having a home."

My father and my mother, of course, didn't see eye to

eye, but my mother never talked him down, so I have no strong feelings about him at all. You hear some people raised the way I am, they don't even want to think about their fathers. I don't have that feeling. In fact, as I've gotten older, I can sort of see him as a person, but I'm not that concerned because my mother did not run him down to us.

They never got a divorce; she did not believe in divorce. My father's biggest problem was alcohol, and my understanding is that if my mother would have agreed that my father could make our living by running a saloon, they might have been together, but for her that was not proper: we were not going to live on the benefits of your downfall as a drinker.

The only things I ever heard my mother say about my father was if I said something funny. Then she would say, "Your father would appreciate that," so I know he must've had a sense of humour. I'd say to her, "Well, did you think it was funny? Did you like it?" She'd say, "I didn't like the content of what you said."

My mother was eighty-eight when she died, and my mother did not let me come into her bedroom when she was getting undressed or into the bathroom when she went into the bathroom. My mother was hopelessly mid-Victorian. I don't know how my mother had my brother and I — I can't even picture it. I'd say that to her, and she'd say, "All right, Bee. Now that's enough of that — now we won't get into that." And I'd say, "What?" and she'd say, "Just leave it alone."

My grandmother was the matriarch; she was the matriarch and her slogan was, "Why do you do so and so? Because I'm Mary Eve Ball. But what reason? I don't have to have a reason: if I don't want to do it, I tell that person that Mary Eve Ball is not going to do it." So that was the end of it.

When I lived with this Aunt Winnie in Cleveland, her sons were older and one of them just adored us. In fact, he looked upon my mother more like an older sister, so he always called her "Sis" because he was closer in age to her. We used to call him "Cousin-Uncle" because he said he was too young for an uncle and too old for a cousin, "so call me Cousin-Uncle," and we did; we grew up calling him Cousin-Uncle Fred.

He had a great romance in his life. He liked — dare I say the word? — a white girl. In the family they didn't say the world wasn't ready yet, but that's what they meant: that the life of a child in a mixed marriage would be too complex. So he married a coloured woman whose mother is white; the wife was a St. Catharines person, and they went to British Columbia, the whole family, and he moved with them, and they were married twenty-five years. When his wife died — I don't know how — he and this same white girl met and married and lived seventeen years happily in British Columbia.

My grandmother died in 1934. I am going to be seventy-seven on the second of October, so I'd be about twenty-four when she died. My grandmother's mother was born in the States. Her father's mother, her grandmother, was born in Madagascar; she was brought over here to this continent as a slave. Her freedom was purchased by a North American Indian chief which we do not know what he was — Mohawk, Cree. He bought her freedom, but when the Fugitive Slave Law was passed over there in the States, it said that any slaves that they could prove are slaves could be captured.[3]

My grandmother's father was afraid for his mother, so

he came from Pennsylvania to Canada and he came to St. Catharines; his name was Jackson and my grandmother's mother name, or maiden name, was Hussey, so that's the end of when they came and how they came here.

Right up until I was married, my grandmother had more or less a say in my life. After my grandfather died — he died in 1925 — my grandmother lived till 1934. That's nine years, and in that time my mother was at her beck and call. Even though I was married in '29 and lived with my husband throughout those years, they were always in and out of my life.

After my grandfather died, my grandmother could not settle down. She tried living with each of these different sons; for all her sort of managing ways, they always liked her because she always opened her heart to everybody when they were in the parsonage. Those doors were open to everybody in Toronto here and when they pastored in London; wherever they pastored that was my grand-mother and grandfather's way, so they had a lot of in and out with people.

I had a very good marriage. Married Clarence Allen in 1929. He was twenty-two and I was eighteen. We were married almost 55 years. As far as satisfaction and what we could achieve in those fifty-four years, we had our ups and downs and those sorts of things. I just have one daughter; I had two, but I lost one when she was seven months old.

My mother was always there. She had always looked after her mother. In the later years my grandmother was paralysed and my mother gave her night and day. I did my best to support her and that, but I didn't always live with them. I did run back and forth. I went to the sanatorium in 1935 and I was in there fourteen months. Tuberculosis. We had moved in to help with my mother and my grandmother, so my mother went in and took charge, and it worked out very well.

We had some very difficult financial times, as far as Blacks were concerned in Toronto. There were no jobs. Mr. Allen was a very dark man and more or less paid the price for that. He'd graduated as an auto mechanic, but, of course, they weren't hiring Black auto mechanics.

When we got married my husband was working at Union Station in the men's washroom — it was staffed with coloured men. Not bad financially, except that my husband was never happy shining shoes. He always felt there was something better. He never wanted to be a porter because he felt you had to take too much — he said he wouldn't last too long because the first fight usually was the end of you and he wasn't going to be called "Boy" or "Sam," so he worked at Union Station as a shoe shine.

He wanted to be a cook on the railroad. He found out that cooks on the railroad were separated from this harassment, so he tried that. But getting on the railroad was a very long process. He started as third cook. But he was on stand-by, so he made up his mind to do the best he could with the shining of shoes. He did that until Imperial Oil.

My uncle was a streetcar motorman in 1924 — that's when they had a conductor and a motorman. He was there because they didn't know he was Black. He didn't look Black — he was totally white in appearance. And my brother, who is a considerably fairer person than I am, he went through the white army when they were not sending coloured soldiers with white soldiers.

In Toronto a lot of organizations had these people all in them, but there was that little, little line. I had a lady say to me, "How come" — we were closer in our later life — "I never really got to know you when we were younger?"

I could have said to her: because at that point you were not coloured. But I didn't say it because it had never bothered me, and what I had to do with her I did. I mean that was her choice.

I had wanted to be a teacher but when I was young there weren't that many Blacks teaching in Toronto. I knew of one, Mr. Jones. Mr. Jones and family by-passed being Black as much as they could, which happened a lot in those days. Mr. Jones was a schoolteacher, and anytime we were trying to make a show of what we had accomplished, Mr. Jones was up there.

Toronto had a lot of prejudice amongst Blacks themselves, they really did, and mostly it was based on colour. There was many of them had good backgrounds — maybe they had a family that was light. If you didn't have this background, but you had the light skin, in Toronto you could move up with whatever it was you were supposed to be that you were doing. Maybe one of the reasons that it never bothered me too much was because my grandmother was a very fair woman, blue eyes, blonde hair.

I have a cousin that was fair, and that meant a lot in the days when we were looking for work — she married the same way I did, her husband's a good brown. She had a job that she wouldn't have had if they had known she was coloured; she was a short-order cook in a variety store, selling over-the-counter candies and doing all the things, and that was up in an area where a lot of coloured people didn't go by much. Of course, this was one of the criticisms that they always made of coloured people: that they always hung around their business places, and they didn't seem to understand that it's a business place, and you didn't go there to sit down and all just because you knew them.

We had a thing in our family about my cousin when she

got her job, which was so much nicer than having to go and do service work or something like that: we just made it our business not to go around her business place, and we didn't feel badly about it or anything — that was the way it was.

Much later, when we bought our second house, which we were in nineteen years out in Scarborough, it was found out that the woman selling us the house had gone around in the neighbourhood to ask if there would be an objection to coloured coming in there because there were no Blacks in there. We moved in there 1960, and even at that time, she passed this hot document around there. I found out about this after. She was buying another house, and she was going to be in the neighbourhood, and she didn't want any ill feeling against herself because she brought in coloured people.

My first job was, as with many Black girls, in service. I had not been in any kind of work, but I felt I could take care of a child, so I took that job. That's what I did prior to marriage, and not for too long, because I would then be sixteen, maybe seventeen. It was Vi Aylestock working at Pemberton's who got me my first mother's helper job. There was a woman there, and she needed a person to look after her daughter, and Vi recommended me.

In service situations I always asked, "Do you hire coloured?" because I did not have financial means to go running up to some place up in Rosedale from where I lived and be turned down when I got to the door — that was carfare spent for nothing. Sometimes they would say, "Well, I'm sorry." Other times I would phone, and they would say, "Well, are you dark?" and I would say, "Well, I'm not dark," and then they might say, "I'm sorry, the reason I'm asking is because we'd like our coloured help to be unquestionably coloured." These were domestic jobs; you were going to live in, in many cases, and they did not want to have their friends or relatives wondering at you.

I guess probably some white people lived with the idea that they would live with a coloured person in their home if they were not extremely dark, and that was because they just keep showing up in their face all the time. Others wanted you to be dark because mostly coming from the States they were accustomed to Black help, and this is what they wanted.

It was when I was trying to find service jobs that this business about being Black came up. Black women had not really had that long of a life in other jobs because it was the war that opened it. The war brought in the necessity for hiring women.

I lived in for maybe one job, but I didn't stay there very long. In a lot of these service jobs you lived in, and you only had Thursday afternoon off and maybe every other Sunday. Some general domestics were doing everything: they were doing the cooking and they were also serving. They were part of the family, but the mistress didn't want any of your life to keep you from getting up early and getting her breakfast.

I was mother's help just before I got married at age eighteen years on December 7, 1929. When I first married I was just unbelievably naive. My husband's idea was that I was married and I was supposed to be at home.

I stayed home during the first year of our marriage and then I had the daughter. In '31–'32 — her first year — I was quite ill and spent some five or six weeks in the hospital and came home from that time. Then I got this opportunity to go work in the shoe factory; once I got into working in the shoe factory then I never went back into domestic service. I never did because I felt I had now an opening tool.

In the shoe factory, which was my first real experience, I was working on the shoes that were all done. They came to the packing bench, and I had to put the insoles in and match shoes and pack them and put them out for shipment. I was on that almost the whole time — a year, two years — and then I was moved up to doing things that required a little skill: making bows, putting bows on shoes. I was used many times to fill in for others in their absence because it seemed I had an ability to take on some other phase, and the same thing applied with the dress factory. When I went into the dress factory I was sent by unemployment insurance. Mr. Switzer was my foreman and very respected; he was a production foreman, which meant he made sure he got the work out right. He didn't take any nonsense or anything like that.

The office just called, and someone said, "Do you hire coloured?" And his answer was, "What the hell do I care what colour they are as long as they do the work?" I was the first Black one in there, and I don't know whether this is why he said it; he had no way of knowing what I was like or anything.

And this was quite often one of the problems that Black people faced in finding the jobs: some people felt you made the application, you should call and give your phone number, and you would call and say, "Do you hire Black?" Sometimes whites, without any hesitation, they would say, "No, I'm sorry."

Before I left, there were other Black people at the dress factory. At the dress factory I started in as an examiner. We got the dresses when they were completely finished: they were brought over on their racks, and our job was to see that everything about them was correct and to take what needed to be done to the operators or the pressers, and I thought this was rather an odd job to put somebody who had not worked with garments.

I ended up being on the draping table, working with the designer. Through different changes in the factory there came a vacancy. They watched me and put me into other situations, and they just decided to give me that start on the draping table, which was not usual unless you went there with some dressmaking training. But I always, always sewed a bit at home and was quite fortunate in that the girl who eventually became the head draper, she liked me; we got along very well, and she felt confident in leaving me at times there doing the job, so when she quit they did not put a head draper on — this is one of the things that happens when you don't have document or something like that. I was like the head draper on the table, I worked with the designer.

When you were on the draping table you got the dress when operators were finished with it and it had been pressed. Now you had been called in, and the designer had shown you a model and shown you how she wanted you to pin that model; it was important that you pinned it, and then it went to the finishers, and they did all this little tacking with thread. If they did not do it where you pinned, or if they did not understand what was required of them, then you could come out with the dress maybe that this shoulder pad wasn't quite even with this one, and that was unacceptable.

The funny part was it went from there to this examiner, which was where I started! As an examiner we got it and you had to say, "This isn't pinned" — you can't say "pinned right" — but you would say, "It goes back to the

examiners, the finishers." And of course their first cry is
"*You* didn't pin it right!" That's factory life, of course.

I had a very great urge to get out of factory life; I found
that it was interesting having a skill, but what I couldn't
seem to take was that people just acted anyway they wanted, and it got to you. I always tried to remember that just
because they weren't ladylike and screamed and hollered
and swore I didn't have to, and that's very difficult to keep
in mind. I left because I really wanted to get out of factories,
and I had a little typing ability because I had gone to night
school.

I left the dress factory to go to work for Carl Woodbeck
— this would be 1948. This was my first job as a married
lady. I took a little drop off in pay when I went to work for
Carl. He came from Owen Sound. He was a person that
had a belief in people that did try to do something for
themselves. He was not a prepossessing-looking person,
but he was sincere in what he did.

Carl had been the church financial collector and he
knew me through church. Then he got this idea to have this
newspaper, *Africa Speaks*.[4] Carl just felt that he could do
this. He would go out to collect funds and then he would
be away from the city for a period of time — he went way
out west — and while he was doing this, he pushed his
newspaper, and he would come back from the west with
50 applications for the paper. At one time we had as many
as 1,000 persons taking it.

And I think it served its purpose. First of all, the name,
of course, made all the coloured people buy it. "Why *Africa
Speaks*?" they would say. I think he felt we all came from
Africa originally, so *Africa Speaks* was what he called it.

The paper ran for quite a while. When I first went there
I was part-time, and I just went in the afternoons and did

these different chores. I filed the cards; the letters came in with the different writers reporting their news. Toronto, London, St. Catharines, Windsor — and, I think, Brantford — had somebody reporting; whatever they wrote, that's what we put in the paper, and he did sort of an editorial.

In the end, he entrusted the whole process to me. I went into the office and part of my duties were to make up the labels for the letters going out. We had the paper printed by a company on King Street, and what I had to do when everything was in — all the city reports — I took it down to this printing company, and they sort of put it together. Then they called me, and I went back down and proofread it for spelling and to be sure it was right to be printed as the paper. We went down and got the paper; it came up to me all laid out, put into bundles of printed paper.

While the paper was away, I was getting the wrappers ready; they were just plain sheets of paper. I had a stencil machine and I had typed the list of addresses. Then I took the paper, ran it through, and the addresses came out through onto this wrapping paper; then you just took the paper and you rolled it up, and you wrapped it up in this paper. We had a glue machine and I glued them. I put them in this wrappers and they went to the post office.

I had gone up to London, and I was looking for work because I had decided that I had to do more than just be part-time with Carl. In London I was staying at my uncle's, but I maintained my home was in Toronto. How I came to go there was because Carl went out on the road to do his collections for the church — that was around May of '50 — and he said to me when he left, "I'm closing the office while I'm gone, but I hope you will come back."

Now here I am trotting up and down, taking this down to the station and getting this printing, and me going running down here and everything. I thought that I could do better, so I'm just going to make an all-out effort. And, in the meantime, we had attempted also to buy our first house, and we just needed more money coming in. I had my mother with me all the time, and that allowed me more freedom of action, even when I was with my own child.

I went into national defence first and national defence did have a union — it was not as big as civilians' society. When I worked for the government, I was in PSAC — the Public Service Alliance of Canada. PSAC was the big one. NDEA, I think, ours was called, National Defence Employees Association. It wasn't as effective as the big one, PSAC.

PSAC was the big one, and once I got into public service — which was the unemployment insurance and old age security — that was the union.

My husband had one idea really: he felt it was his place to make the money. If he had had his way, I would never have worked. That is not to say that I wouldn't have — my one real wish was to be a school teacher, and I think if my life had've gone differently, if that was possible during my time as a Black, then I would have.

I worked because there was a financial need to work. I bought things and my husband just did not make enough money; he did not have what he called "financial security" until he got into Imperial Oil around 1941.

He got in because whenever they called, he went. Also, he was given credit for the fact that he supplied: if a man wanted a day off, he would call and ask if Clarence could come in. That was set pay: it didn't matter if it rained or what it did, you worked. I would say this situation went on two to three years. Imperial Oil counted that time as part of his service.

It was messenger work. Imperial Oil headquarters was at 56 Church Street and all they hired was coloured men. But it was not shoeshine, it was not railroad: it was employment and it was good employment. They never did have a union, but they did always have good work relations.

There was a group of women — my grandmother was one of the group — and they set up the Eureka.[5] They were women who did not necessarily have to work — quite a few of their husbands were on the railroad. They were women who liked their social life and they could afford to have a little get-together. I think that they played cards — not that it was talked about much. Now at that time, all ministers' wives were asked to be members. My grandmother did not play cards very much, but she did join, and she's in the original picture of the persons that formed the club. We had a very beautiful seventieth anniversary, and at that time they had a picture display, and that picture of the original ladies was there.

The Eureka Club was founded in 1910. I always remembered that mother said that they had twenty members, and my mother was president of it for one year. They sent out mail and things like that, did little kindnesses. They were a social club when they first were formed, and they were very proud of the fact it wasn't too long before they all sat back and said we ought to be doing something worthwhile, and there were many things they did. For instance, they sent Christmas baskets to the needy, and that grew into quite a thing, but it has gone down, of course. At this moment I run the birthday register which they set up.

I joined the Eureka Club before my mother died, so it had to be before '69 — my mother died in '69. I can remember attending meetings long before I joined and attending meetings when they used to meet at Mrs.

Thompson's — Melvin Simpson's grandmother. I think we have at this point seven members maybe, and we feel that this is where the young people should be taking this club; we feel that because the club is so old and struggled so long, it would be nice if the young people — the daughters of these members — would have felt that it was important to them.

In the Eurekas we had a definite feeling — a poor feeling, I felt — about doing things with white women. Two of our members had said at one time they had had white women ask to join, and one was a very dominant personality and said that we were Eureka, a Black organization, and that we had been a Black organization all these years. She thought that whatever we achieved was that we did it as Black women. The other member dropped out eventually, but she said that all her life she'd been going around fighting more or less to say we are no different, we aren't different, we can do as much as them and all the rest of it, so what was wrong with us having a white join us? And the other member was adamant that we are a Black club; we only joined together with white women for women's day of prayer. We went and met, joined their church; we did not go and run a counter day of prayer.

We had a very good organization that I was a member of at one time; it was called the Coloured Women's Council. The lady who organized it — Mrs. Sarah Clarke — she lived here in Toronto. She had this dream that she was forming this Coloured Women's Council and it was supposed to be seniors, juniors and intermediates. Grace Trotman and myself, we were in charge of the juniors, and mother and Mrs. Hazel Pitman were in charge of the intermediates. Of course, the seniors looked out for themselves. The juniors were the girls, and their older sisters were in the intermediate group, and the seniors were the mothers.

Most of the Eurekas belonged to it. This was her idea of getting coloured women organized to be somebody in the community; that's what they did, which is probably what Congress of Black Women is doing now.

We would just have the children come to meetings on a certain day, and they put on a concert or something. Grace was a musician, and we kept them meeting and doing things and having things in themselves that kept them off the street — these were girls, of course.

We had always been making the children feel that this was a group that they could aspire to, and then, when the time came, they would be in the Coloured Women's Council. I can't really put my finger on the demise of that organisation. It sort of just faded away — Mrs. Clarke took sick and left Toronto, and we went along with the three groups still functioning.

I was never involved in the group that Kay Livingstone organized.[6] At the time that was formed — the way it was explained to me — if your husband was not professional, you were not considered. I found out that many of the members, their husbands were just railway men.

At one time I was a musician in the Eastern Star; the Eastern Star is the female end of the masonic organization — these are Black Masons I'm talking about. Of course, the background of the Star is not so much to be a social club as it is to be a builder of womanhood; it's supposed to teach you the things and you are supposed to absorb them and apply them in your life — all the important things that go to make good womanhood.

Being in it, I think, really and truly does help to improve you; it does because if you take any part of it seriously —

if it even just inspires you while you're at the meetings — the ritual and everything does sort of inspire you. I don't ever go out to one of their services, or whatever, without having a good feeling when it's over that I'm part of that. I try to remind myself to be part of it all the time.

I'm a missionary person. At one point missionary society was a women's part of the church. They seemed to be concerned that women were missionaries, and yet there's always been male missionaries, so I don't know how we accomplished it.

The BME used to have a literary society and in that society I think that we did fairly well. I was assistant art editor. Verda Cook was the art editor and she was good.

It seems as though in all these small and busy-seeming groups that I have worked with that there is a sort of determination there to keep women playing a part on their own in the community. Whether it's a conscious feeling or not, I don't know; I can't recall that I heard it said in their constitutions or anything like that. I guess I never felt that women are unequal to men. I've always felt that that might be what somebody else set it up as, but we women are quite capable of doing most things that men do.

Notes

1. Richard Ball was a leading figure in the BME Church. See Winks, *op. cit.*, p. 358.

2. *The Evening Telegram*, Toronto, n.d.

3. The Fugitive Slave Law, passed in the United States in 1850, allowed for the recapture of slaves who had fled to the northern states.

4. Winks says that the paper started "slightly later" than 1953, but Bee Allen puts the date at 1948. See Winks, pp. 404 and 408–409.

5. Mary Ball was one of the original members of the Eureka Club.

6. The Canadian Negro Women's Association, also known as the Negro Women's Club, was founded in 1951 with Kay Livingstone as president, Aileen Williams as recording secretary and Audrey Grayson as treasurer. See Rella Braithwaite, *The Black Woman in Canada* (Toronto, self-published, 1976).

Saxonia Shadd
1912

I was born in 1912. My people came to Canada around the 1840s.

I don't know too much about my mother's mother. They were not slaves; I don't know too much about them except that they had found their way up here. They came from the Baltimore, Maryland area.

On my mother's mother's side, one of my grandmother's sisters married a freeman who had made his way down from Halifax. He was being brought over from Africa, and when he was on board ship they stopped in Virginia. There he saw a flag — a ship flying the British flag — and I don't know how he knew, but he knew that that was a British ship, and he slid overboard and swam over to the ship. The captain picked him up and brought him to Halifax as he was coming there.

I don't know anything at all about my father's people. He was from Virginia. I only know that he was an only child. But as near as I can establish, they was pretty well freeborn, most of them. My grandmother on my mother's side was freeborn, and I don't know how they came this way — I don't know how they ended up here.

My grandmother on my mother's side, she was Mary Anderson, daughter of John Anderson and Louisa Johnston. She was the first cousin of Perry Osborn, who was involved in Harper's raid.[1] My mother used to say Perry was at Harper's Ferry and I paid no attention to it till I started looking. I had my grandmother's picture. Arlie Robbins said she was the spitting image of Osborn Anderson, so I sent my grandmother's picture down to her, and she said I even took the hair growing and the same lines back on the forehead. She said she took a magnifying glass to it and the likeness is unmistakeable.

My grandmother died young, had twenty-one children, twenty-one on a small farm. I can only name about sixteen or seventeen of them; that's all I can name. I know my younger uncles on the tail end of the family, just what my mother told me. My mother was third from the last; of course, my grandmother buried two sets of twins. My grandmother was dead long before I was born. She died young.

My mother was born right here at Shrewsbury and she was buried in 1880. She was the third from the end, and my uncle Joe was the first coloured porter on the CPR when it first opened, the CPR railroad that ran Montreal-Toronto, Toronto-Vancouver. He ran out across the Prairies.

Uncle Joe was a big kind of good-looking guy. He and another porter, they got out west there somewhere in the Winnipeg area — largely Indian encampments out there — and I guess they get to courting some of these girls, and the courting got too intense. One night the breeze got behind them, and he and Uncle had to swim the Assiniboine River at one point!

When my father died my mother kept up a small farm. She worked as a housemaid and helped do house cleaning and things of that sort, anything to keep bread in our mouths. We raised tobacco and beans, stuff like that from an early age. We had to go in the field. She did it all, except what help she could get — we had to have somebody come and hoe, come and weed it all.

My mother supported us all by herself. We helped at home, hoeing and all in the fields, but also we worked over on Ariel Marsh's, pulling weeds, weeding onions. We made a dollar a day. Phillip, my brother, started at fifty cents a day, but I was younger when I started. I got a dollar a day, and we worked from seven in the morning to six at night, and then at the very last I remember that in the third or fourth summer we got up to two dollars a day. The work was hard; you worked on your knees all day long.

Don't tell me about tobacco, I've done everything you have to do about tobacco. I've planted tobacco; I've hoed tobacco; I've suckered tobacco — you've got those little suckers you've got to bend down all the way and break them off. I've cut the tobacco down, and I've helped the leaves put on a long steel pole and put them over there — they call it needling. I've needled tobacco, and I've baled tobacco, and I've helped to hang it in the barn. I've done everything you could do with tobacco.

My mother ran the farm with whoever she could get to help. Since an early age — soon as we could lift the hoe right — we were in the field hauling out the weeds and stuff. She was very determined, very determined not to be beaten down. She had her opinions. She wanted us all to be educated and she wouldn't let anything stand in the way.

Grandpa saw to it that they all had the common school education to grade eight — my grandfather was long dead before any one of us was born, but Grandpa helped to instill those values in her that education was the prime concern. She was bound that we were going to have an education, so my brother and I both finished high school. I went on to teacher's college, and he dropped out of school and worked, helped to pay for it.

My brother went into the electrical engineering and when the war was on he was with the Royal Canadian Engineers — he did their field telephones and their inter-communications stuff. Because he had a bad leg the people that he worked for in Blenheim, they wrote all kinds of letters to members of Parliament. They wouldn't let him go. They said they had to keep him here. He never had to go overseas, but they had him in Halifax. Ship-to-shores and all that kind of stuff — he had to do that in the army.

If we had not been so poor, he would've been able to go to school, and I feel that he would have made a skilled electrical engineer; he had the gift for it.

I wanted to be a doctor, and because I was a girl my uncle wouldn't help me — the one that was a doctor. He wanted my brother to be a doctor. My brother couldn't stand the sight of blood, but nothing fazes me! He didn't want to pay for my education. My mother couldn't pay and he wouldn't pay for it. He said, "No, she's a girl. She doesn't need it." That's what they thought back then. So, of course, I became the only other thing — a teacher — that was open at that particular time. If it had been days like this, I'd have been going to medical school.

I went to teacher's college. It was called normal school then, London Normal School. I had no problems, but where someone might've had a problem, I didn't have any problem because I just assumed that there was no dif-ference. But I have to say that I never was conscious of being a different colour or anything of that sort, so I

must've gone with a really good bunch. I never socialized
except with the school activities. The young men always
came and asked me to dance and all that, and I was invited
over to two of the girls' boarding houses to come over and
sit and chat.

My mother, though, was very outspoken. She never
allowed anybody to put her down. She let everybody know
that she was as good as any of them and better than most
of them. She knew how to carry herself and she worked
like a dog to keep food in our mouths.

There is a story about her and the church. The slip the
minister made that time, and all she did was she got up
and gave him a hard, hard look. He said, "There's a nigger
in the woodpile," and it was a slip. He didn't mean it; he
wasn't that kind of person. He was a white minister — they
used to come through. We were a small congregation, and
we didn't have a regular minister, and the minister used to
come out from Blenheim every Sunday. It was just a slip.

When the preacher said that my mother didn't say
anything; she just looked. She gave him a look! She gave
him a look that would open a clam — my daughter, Sharon,
always says, "Now Mother, you inherited grandmother's
look!" I used to be able to look down at the kids in school
and everything got quiet. They'd say, "Look it, that old
lady would be able to shrivel a snake!"

She looked at him — she stood right up in her place —
and she threw up her head, and she laughed and walked
out the door. That was it. He told Mr. Thompson, who was
taking him back to Glen Allan, "I'd sooner lost my right
arm than to do what I did today."

He was true blue, but that expression you use it without
meaning. The person is not prejudiced, it's just a saying
that they've heard. But you could do the same thing about

maybe an Italian. One time I almost goofed: somebody came in my store here, all loaded down with a lot of bags; I was on my way to say, "What's happening? You look like a dago on his way back to Italy." He was standing with his bags — and I just skinned it. I know how easy it is to say things, so I really didn't take umbrage at that. I know it wasn't meant maliciously.

I went to normal school and graduated. I taught first in Shrewsbury. After I got married I used to supply here at Buxton. I taught for a while at Harrow. Shrewsbury was a mixed school, and I think when I went to Harrow there was no whites there at that time. As a matter of fact, they were extremely prejudiced there because I was going to get some pop and they said, "You can't go in there. You can go and buy the pop and take it out, but you can't drink it here." It was very prejudiced.

I taught in Shrewsbury and Harrow, and I ended up in Blenheim which was all white — there was no coloured families lived there at all. Now coloured families worked there and they had an abiding respect for each other. The people that was born in Blenheim had a great respect. Our mailman from Shrewsbury — several people worked for him, and looked up to him and respected him. We had a very good relationship; nobody was ever conscious of colour there.

Teaching in these schools was all fairly routine. The last years that I taught — I went back to it after my youngest child was in high school — they were short on teachers and I went back. The school at that time was half and half, half-coloured and half-white. The population had shifted that much.

I should've been about twenty-three when I got married in 1936. When we taught we were expected to resign when we got married back then. It didn't bother me, because I couldn't handle both jobs. I married a storekeeper. My first child was born a year and seven months after I was married. And I had a family — I married somebody who had two little boys in the first place. He had two little boys from his first marriage. His wife died young, and his third child was a baby and, of course, the baby died. I was housekeeping and child-rearing and helping out some here in the store.

After the children were small, he decided to go and raise his own meat. He raised quite a bit of meat. Way back through at the back, he built sort of a barn and raised calves and pigs and stuff like that. He was busy with that then, and then he switched over, and he went over into custom work, threshing.

Custom work they called it in those days — where you worked for the people with the threshing machines. Nowadays, everybody has their own combines, but then they had the machines, and people all came and worked together. They moved the machine to another farm and all the farmers would come and help.

Ira ran a threshing machine and he used to work here and out in Chatham Township. He'd get up at five in the morning and cut the meat and stuff, then I would come out and take over — bring the baby in the high chair, the current baby — and then take care of the store. That sort of thing. Then in '59 I went back into full-time teaching school and taught from then continuously to '72.

I was in Shrewsbury first and then they consolidated the schools. I was in a one-room, eight-grade school. Then they consolidated them and moved up to Blenheim. But when I was there, just before I went back full-time, Ira decided that the young people here needed something here to get them going. He always was a music lover, so he had this idea of forming a band. So everybody, of course, says, "You can't do it." And being a Shadd, they say you can't do it, that means he was going to do it, come hell or high water.

He went around; he gathered up all second hand instruments — he had several of them himself — so he got this band going. Then they had to have practice. They had to have somebody to keep track of who came and who didn't come, so that became another little side job for me. That was '53. I helped with that, and at times he had to be away with the band I had to be at the store, because you always had to have somebody in the store.

At first, he hired a teacher, but that took money, and then he learned to play the other instruments himself, and then he taught the kids — he played a violin, saxophone.

He used to play with big orchestras in Cleveland, but when his father died he came home and took over the family; at twenty-seven he became the father to his younger brothers and sisters, the William Shadd family. He even had Grandfather Garrison teaching him to play the baritone. The two of them used to be sitting in there, Grandfather would say, "Oomm pah pah, oomm pah pah," that sort of thing.

But he got everybody involved: the trombone — anything like that he learned so he could pass the knowledge on to the other kids. He taught himself and then taught it to everybody. He just had this burning desire to make it go and that took up a lot of time.

I was at home at that time. I was always here to keep the store for him. You know what it is with a country store: somebody wanders in now and again, and one thing and another. Saturday afternoons usually everybody is in town.

To raise money we used to hold square dances. I used to MC the square dances and so I got into square-dance calling. We made money at that, and everybody got involved, our friends at different places. We raised money to buy instruments and to outfit the band and that sort of thing. All through the winter, every other Friday night, we used to have square dances. We had the money for that and the band's parents would help with different details.

When I was in the hospital seven years ago for my knee operation I met up with this nurse — and she wanted to know my history, and she wanted to know how I'm recovered, and do you have a hobby? And gave me a look that meant that tap dancing and shooting craps. And I said, "Yes, I have a hobby. I'm a call girl." She almost flipped her wig. Then in the end — the poor thing, she looked so hard — just to put her out of her misery I said, "Well, I call for square dances. Where I come from, I'm known as that call girl from North Buxton," and I let her heart beat!

Got picked for the best band at the parade. At the International Freedom Festival, we were the only coloured band there. On one occasion we played for the Shriners in Detroit. That's when one of the horns got stolen. It was Violet Shadd's clarinet. The kids were hanging around, and they got the horns filed while they were waiting for the parade to start. And we played in Detroit twice; they had us play for a Tiger's ball game, for intermission and before the game started. We played all over, played for the Queen in Windsor. They went to Sarnia, Thamesville, Amherstburg.

During those years of the band and all, I was the go-fer, and in '59 I went back to teaching full-time. I used to drive up to Shrewsbury every day, but when it came time for the band, I used to wash and iron. Every time that band went out — and it went out at least once a week — ten shirts, ten band shirts. I went to school for a rest in the fall.

When the schools consolidated I said, "Maybe I won't go. Maybe it's time for me to move on to something else to help out at home." But the United Church minister from Giles came to the school one day, and he said, "Mrs. Shadd, I've heard you may not move up to the big school. Why?" He had this in the back in his mind that maybe there was something.

I said, "No, I just thought maybe they were going to change, and I just thought maybe it was time for the change in one of the older teachers." He said, "I wouldn't want to hear that. Promise me that you'll go." I was half-way leaning towards it, and I said, "All right, I'll go." I'm the one that brought culture to the institution.

I guess I could say that I was a leader in several enterprises. I had good ideas in several things. Every month a teacher had to put up an exhibit up in the front hall of something they were doing in their class. Mine took the prize for the best exhibit twice, and like that I got along very well.

When the schools consolidated I moved up to Blenheim and stayed there until Ira was sixty-five. They said that he couldn't have the post office there anymore. He said, "Let it go," but I knew that would've hurt him badly because it would mean closing the store and one thing and another. That would've been hard for him, so I said I'm going to quit and I did. I resigned so I could become the new postmaster, and then it could stay here in the store because they would've taken the post office away from the village.

I finally retired in 1972. I came to take over the post office. I would've still been teaching if it hadn't been for that. I substituted teaching. I had a way with kids that were difficult. I don't know why — I guess it takes one to know one. A lot of the young people, they have things they're troubled over, things that happen in school. They come in and talk it out with me, so I feel very good about that.

My life has been very ordinary. To me it has — I haven't done as some people do; some people are people of letters and all that sort of thing, but not me. I'm just part of the community. I still have the store, but I don't do too much of anything extra — I fool around with the piano, mostly I don't do too much. I taught myself.

I gave birth to three children, but we had the five because already two were my husband's. My kids at school called Ira the Music Man. They called him the Bubble Gum Man too because he used to bring them bubble gum and not tell me. He'd leave it in the school yard and draw a map as to where to find it. He just used to go by on the half-day on the Wednesday 'cause I had a cousin that was a semi-invalid that would come out. He would ride with me, but during the day when we were all in school he would do this. He said, "Don't tell her. Don't let her know a thing." I remember when he was sick the first time and they sent him a card, and when I was picking the cards after, he came home and he had a card from the kids that said Mr. Bubble Gum Man, Mr. Ira Shadd, but inside it has, "Don't let on to you know who."

I never thought about being a Black woman one way or another. I'm just a woman and colour has nothing to do with it. I guess I've always been that way all my life; I haven't thought in terms of achievement and colour. I have not been discriminated against as a Black woman, never, never. As a woman, I don't think so. I've been one of the fortunate ones: I've never come up against discrimination. I don't really know why except that if discrimination was lurking in the background, I failed to recognize it. I wasn't expecting to be discriminated against, therefore I didn't look for it. I've had very good rapport with all kinds of people around here. All white people — they've all been all around here — used to come to the store. When they put the 401 in they cut off a lot of farms back here that used to come in here. Now I get some people off the eighth and ninth concessions. As a matter of fact, I get more trade from white people than I do from coloured. They patronize me more than my own.

I hang those signs up about women's lib just to liven up the place. I just do that to get the fellows going and I never put them up until winter. Just to make the dull winter go. And they say, "What've you got there now?" One day, my sign fell down — it had some of that stuff on it and it fell down — and they came and asked where it was. But that doesn't mean a thing: I just like to needle them. I just like to kid everybody; it's just part of me — that just gives them something to yak about.

A couple of years ago it was a dull winter, and I thought: I'll put that up. They did more yelling, and Gary, he tried to alter my sign. I'll say, "You're the only male here; therefore you're in the wrong," that sort of thing. Then they come back to argue the point, and it gives them something to do in a quiet dull time, but I have no feelings about it.

As a matter of fact, you couldn't call me strictly a women's libber because I like men to do things for me: I like them to open the car door, I like them to hold the door for me, I like them to do all the paying — all that, especially the paying part. But I believe in women's lib to this extent: that I think that if you work you should get equal pay, and I think that you should not be discriminated against. I refuse to be inferior, but I'm not a women's libber.

When I read about this rescue here off Halifax when the oil rig ,went down — these people were all in the rig; they were all taken out in the lifeboat, twenty-five men and two women — I thought: what in heaven's name is a woman doing out there on an oil rig? I don't have to prove it, I know who I am. I don't have to prove it to anyone. If they don't know through my actions, and if they don't know what commitment to what project I'm in from the way I carry myself, then too bad for them.

Notes

1. According to Winks, *op. cit.*, pp. 266–269, U.S. citizen John Brown had held a meeting of abolitionists in Chatham in May 1858:

    > What transpired at the convention is not clear. Meeting in the First Baptist Church on May 8 and 10, giving out that the were organizing a Negro Masonic Lodge, twelve white and thirty-four black men — at first under the chairmanship of William C. Munroe, a Negro — apparently discussed guerilla warfare against slave holders. (Martin R.) Delany (a Black doctor and advocate of relocation to West Africa), who cochaired the session insisted that Harper's Ferry was never mentioned, but others — Israel Shadd of the Provincial Freeman, J.H. Kagi ... Osborn P. Anderson ... and Reverend Thomas M. Kinnaird ... later suggested otherwise....

    Brown's group hit Harper's Ferry, Virginia on October 17, 1859, but he was captured and subsequently executed. Osborn Perry Anderson fled to Canada after the raid. Later, Mary Ann Shadd prepared Anderson's papers for publication.

June Robbins
1913

I was born April 20, 1913. My mother was born in 1881, my grandmother in 1864. Now my grandmother, she was a Spaniard, I know that much. I never heard them say where she came from.

I was one of the younger ones; I don't know as much as the older ones would know. I was born in the North Buxton area, on the eighth concession.

My father was born here. I got a paper with all that on it. I can't remember way back, but my ancestors came as fugitives. My great-grandfather was a slave.

My mother's people came from Kentucky. My mother was born in Kentucky, and then she finished high school and college. My mother was seventeen when they moved to Cleveland. She had three brothers and two other sisters besides, and they were all educated in Cleveland. When my sister and I were about ten to twelve years old, they took us to Cleveland and they taken us to Simpson. We had relatives in Simpson, Ohio and Oberlin, Ohio. They taken us all through Ohio to our relatives.[1]

My mother, she sang all the time. Charlie Robbins, he used to come over there all the time and he'd sing with her.

They learned us all kinds of songs and everything. We used to hang on my mother! Because we used to figure that my mom would let us do things that our father wouldn't. Our father was strict, so you could get around your mother more than you could your dad.

My father ran on the railroad, and my mother had seven of us. She looked after all her children, all us little ones. The government didn't help you like they help all these children. We all had to work. My mother didn't work outside the house; she had enough job looking after seven.

We had a garden where we grew all the vegetables. We had chicken, geese, ducks, so we never had to buy. Never had to buy. That's why I tell these children they have it easy — they're walking around all summer — and we didn't walk around. You'd go to school in the morning; when you come home at night, you went in and changed your clothes from school, you pick up the hoe, and you go out there in the garden till supper time. Your mother'd call you in for supper time. After supper time, if you got your work done, they let you go play ball.

My sister and I belonged to the girls' ball team. We both wanted to play ball at night. At times we'd go hoe in the garden and we'd have the dishes clean. This night we'd go over and play ball early. We washed all the dishes, cleaned up the kitchen, but we hid all the pots and pans. My mother — when she got ready to cook the next day — couldn't find no pans hardly. They looked: everything was dirty. My mother and my grandmother left them dirty. My sister and I that night, we were hurrying to try and get through the dishes, and when we looked around, my mother and grandmother had all these pans we had dirty. They brought them all out and put 'em right there! So we never tried that one again!

We all worked. It's just been this last thirty years that the children haven't had to work as hard as what we worked when we come along. Four boys and three girls. The boys had to milk cows, and we'd always pray the boys wouldn't have to go away 'cause when the boys went away we'd have to milk. But these children have it easy, they just run up and down the roads and have a good time!

When we got big enough, all of us, we'd go get hoes and we'd go into each place. We'd ask the man does he want his field sowed. We sowed corn, beans, hoed the wheat — that's the way we earned money because we didn't get no allowance from the government, nothing at all. Only thing you got was what you worked for. We picked up potatoes, we picked tomatoes, and we rode planters. Two of us sit on the back, and a man would drive the tractor. Before they had the tractor they had horses: we'd sit on them planters. We planted everything. The way you'd do it was every time the planter would click, you'd put a tomato plant and that'd be two or three rows at a time — and we did tobacco, tomatoes, cabbage plants.

We all attended right up there at the Buxton school. When we went to school it wasn't divided at all like now. There was just one row. We'd be eighty-four in that school. Mr. Alexander, he'd give two years of high school.

The main one learned us to sing by note was Mr. Alexander. He'd have a mandolin, and he'd get out that mandolin, and he'd make you stand up by your seat, and you'd have to do the scales. You'd have to come down, and you'd have to go up, and if you made a mistake!

After, the school was divided — they said there was too many children for him to look after. They divided the school after they got two teachers, and he give two years of high school, him and the other teachers. Lot a children that wouldn't leave, wouldn't go to a high school. There they'd get two years of high school. I just started the high school.

I went one month in high school, and my brother had taken spinal meningitis, and I taken care of my brother for four years. He had spinal meningitis and, at that time, the nurses didn't come out in the country — you couldn't get a nurse to come out in the country, so somebody had to look after. There was another boy — he took spinal meningitis on Sunday and he died on Wednesday. Everybody was scared around here 'cause they thought what he had was catching. They thought what my brother had was the same kind.

I took care of him just like a nurse. I worked under just a young doctor — he just come out of school. He was from Merlin; he come from Toronto down this way, but he was just out of school. The only thing, I'd never make a nurse: when he sticked those needles, I covered my eyes. If a person had spinal meningitis, they stick those needles in your neck and they draw it out. They draw that serum out, and then they take that serum, and they put goat serum and sheep serum. They'd draw so much liquid out and they put that liquid in. I'd never make a nurse. I had to massage my brother. I rubbed him most of the time with oils. We had snake oil, skunk oil — every kind of oil — and they kept him massaged to keep those muscles. His head was way back here — you'd be surprised how far a person's neck can stretch.

I taken care of my brother for four years. He came out okay. He started walking — we had a hard time getting him to walk. We had a chair, something that had rollers on them, that old type of chairs — they had rollers on them. I put him on the chair and I put it on the sidewalk. My father helped me carry a big stone in the chair, and I used to lean my brother against this chair and push him up and down the sidewalk. That's the way he learned to walk again. Just like a baby starting to walk again. That's why I say children of today, they have no idea. All them using all this drug and everything — they don't know half of it!

After my brother got better, I still stayed home 'cause it'd taken over the four years. We looked after him, and looked after him, and then exercised and massaged him, and then he got so he could walk.

He worked for a number of years. Then his back commenced to bothering him. He went to Ann Arbor and had an operation. After he had this operation, his back give out on him. He just started going down and he got so he couldn't walk at all. Before he died they had him in the hospital.

I got a job in Chatham. We worked at Libby's plant in Chatham. We worked in there, did a little bit of everything — peeling all kinds of vegetables on an assembly line. We worked in there, me and my sisters, again when World War II was on. We all worked in there. All the food was dehydrated and that's the way they sent it overseas. I did a little bit of everything. While the war was on they were short of men. We used to pitch hay, go out in the fields and pitch hay. They'd take two women to make one man! That little bit of hay a woman could throw — we couldn't throw as much as a man could throw up on the load.

We worked shift work. In Chatham we would find odd jobs on the farms. In later years, we all worked the fruit farm out on number three concession. We picked fruit there. I wouldn't dare do that now. When you're young you don't think about things — the way the young people are with cars, they don't think about danger. After, you get

older and sit and realize. We'd climb those trees on tall
ladders. We didn't think nothing of them. We picked cher-
ries, pears, peaches, blueberries, crab apples, all kinds of
fruit. My brother that's younger than I am worked on the
railroad. The other two brothers worked at Campbell's
Soup, and then before they went to Chatham, they worked
around on the farms.

Mansfield, my nephew, would just be eleven years old.
Garrison had the place up on the tenth. It had rained and
when he got up he realized all the men he had working
had gone home. He didn't have nobody to drive the tractor
home. He had the car and the tractor and he wondered
how he was going to drive it. He let Mansfield drive — we
had a fit!

He was only eleven years old. We hunted and hunted
for Mansfield, asked everybody — nobody saw him! One
of my brothers happened to be home, and he was over
there on the Front Street, and said who come down the
road sitting rear back but Mansfield! Like he was driving
a Cadillac! He's sitting driving this tractor. He'd only be
eleven years old!

When we come along for the summer there'd be as
many children out of town come into Buxton as there were
all of us in Buxton. That's the way they did when we come
along. Everybody would open up their house and take all
these children in. They'd come up here for the summer —
and the roads used to be just full of children — and they
never got in no trouble because we never had any police
out here. There wasn't no police out here. The only time
we saw the police was maybe there'd be an accident, but
the children never got in any trouble.

We used to walk up and down the roads. Mr. Shadd had
the threshing machines. They'd be threshing up to Mrs.

Shadd's, and we'd walk up to Mrs. Shadd's, whole bunch
of us. Those folks! At that time you didn't play; if you went
up there, they'd put you to work. We used to go and we
used to just go for the fun of it. We'd go in, and some would
set the tables, and they'd have you peeling potatoes, and
they'd have you peeling apples — them old people believed in working, and if you went they'd put you right to
work.

The children would all be leaving for the summer; we'd
all get together, and we'd have a party some place, and the
girls would bring cookies and sandwiches, and the boys
would bring ice cream. We'd have a great big party for all
these children before they left Buxton. That's the way we
spent time.

In the wintertime we used to skate. They had the old
pond back there, and the boys used to get the shovels and
brooms and go back and clean it off. They'd skate and
that's the way we spent all our time. There was forty-four
boys and forty-two girls when I come along in Buxton.
That's the way they formed the Dramatic. The hall over the
tracks! We gave enough dances to build that hall. We'd
walk from here up to South Buxton, girls and boys, and
we'd clean the hall and everything — get it all ready and
have a dance. It was just a few people; then pretty soon it
got known. People used to come from all over — Pontiac,
Ann Arbor — come up there and dance and party. They'd
all come up there. Boys would ask you to go up to the
dance with you. They'd have to come to the house to pick
you up, take you up to the dance. The boy had to come to
the house and meet the parents before you'd be allowed to
go out with him. I didn't go out to a dance by myself till I
was nineteen.

Archie Prince and my brother and a whole bunch of

them, they'd all dress and go up there to South Buxton to white dances, and they wouldn't let them go into the dance to dance with the white girls. When we'd have a dance the white boys would want to come in, and the boys would close the door; they wouldn't let them in either.

When we worked in Chatham in the Libby's factory, we worked side by side with all the white women. After the war, all the country people had to leave all the factories and come back. We did other jobs and then they hired the people from the city of Chatham. A lot of us worked on farms around here. A lot of women went to the fruit orchards out on Highway 3, the fruit farms. We all worked out there. There used to be a great big truck used to come down here. All the bunch came out to the fruit farm. You'd get much more than you'd get for a day's work. It's according to how you picked: if you picked steady all day, you'd make good. But a lot of time a lot of them their legs was tired.

I was in my twenties. I worked the summer in the fields, picking the fruit, in the winter working in Chatham; I worked for a doctor for fifteen years. I took care of his baby. His wife was sick; she had to go to Arizona. They had three little bad boys and I took care of them. I stayed there till his little girl started for school. My mother told me I better come home 'cause the little girl gets so attached to me she wouldn't want me to never leave and come home. I left and come home and I went out to the fruit farm. I worked out at the fruit farm for a long time.

A lot of women went out to the cornfields. Here in Chatham they come out in the country, and they pick tomatoes, and a lot of them suckered corn in the spring. You go along and take the little riffs that come out in the corn — you break them off so the ears grow. Women worked in the corn; then they worked in the plants in Chatham.

I moved to Chatham in 1944. I went to work doing housework. The people I worked for decided to build a marina, and they built a marina at Wallaceburg. I worked at the marina for quite a few years. Twenty-five years.

I was an inspector; all I did was walk. I'd walk all day: upstairs, downstairs, and everything. The inspector is around there so you have to do your job. That's what I told them: anybody I catch, I had books in my pocket.

The people that owned the marina, they kept all the doors locked and they only had one door. All the workers had to pass through to come in, and I stood with the hairnets at the door — everybody had to put on a hairnet. If you said you didn't want a hairnet on, you couldn't come in to work. Anybody that worked there, you had to have your hair covered, the men too; they couldn't come in the kitchen if not. Everybody had to wear uniforms; it didn't matter what kind of dress. Even the boss's wife, didn't matter what kind of dress she had on, she had to put on a white coat.

I was living in Chatham and working in Wallaceburg. Thirty-four miles a day; it was seventeen miles out there and seventeen miles back. Black people couldn't stay there after dark. They were prejudiced. A man came to fix the stove and he made some cracks about black and everything. Mr. Fiddler, the man who owned the place, just shooed him out. He called over to where he was working at the cab company. He told them not to send him over there no more. They were bad out there. I didn't have no problems; he just made the remarks.

Then they had an immigration fellow — he was coloured too — come over there because some of the folks hadn't reported in on the boat. They kept track of all the boats when they come in, and lots of boats didn't go to immigration. They'd call and give them the numbers to immigration over there. This coloured fellow he come in — and I knew he was coloured 'cause he had little curls, he'd try and pass for white — and he was really nasty. I didn't say nothing; I didn't say nothing to the boss, but the boss was sitting listening to what he was saying. He treated me badly. I got a lot of that, but when you're working you just have to — you got a lot of that in Wallaceburg, every place.

One time the boats come in early and I was walking around there. Miss Hazel Horn was an inspector too. We have the girls get everything ready. Something was wrong with the meat cutter, so we couldn't cut the meat. Mr. Fiddler, he says to Miss Horn, "You and June take the meat and go over to the butcher's shop." We went over to the butcher's shop, and people were coming and going and coming and going. Miss Horn was sitting waiting for me in the car. The man served everybody coming and going, and he never even asked me, "Is there something you want?" or anything. I stood with my meat, and stood and stood. Miss Horn, she says I was in so long she come to see what was wrong. People come and gone — and they served everybody — then, when the store was empty, they served me quiet. They were nasty out there. It made you feel awful and you couldn't say nothing.

I didn't want to start no trouble, me the only one out there. They had a coloured cook. The coloured cook was just as nasty as the white ones were out there. He was married, for one thing, and his wife was born blind. He had all these white girls out there, and I guess he was scared I was going to tell on him. It didn't matter to me; I told him you could have them upstairs, downstairs — just as long as they don't bother me, I ain't bothered by what you do.

Who said there was no race mixing at that time? There's always been and you know what I tell people? There's been just as much prejudice even out here — even right out here in the country — only it's not as extensive as it is in the city.

Wallaceburg's always been prejudiced, same way Tilbury. Years ago — I'd be about seventeen — I went down to Tilbury and they had a little theatre now. The little theatre was hardly as big as anything. We'd get a whole bunch of us young people — we all went down there to this theatre on Sunday night for the midnight show. When we first start in the man wasn't going to let us in. After we bought the tickets, he wasn't going to let us in! The boys that was with us, they just pushed by this little fellow and went on in. And when we got to laughing in the show, this little usher he come down — he was going to put us out. Some of the boys they were dudes, and some of the boys said, "It would take more than you. It'd take more than you to put us out."

That was years ago. They've always been prejudiced. Same way Merlin used to be prejudiced: coloured people could go there; coloured people could go up there and you could buy groceries — and a lot of them would talk to you and everything — they wanted you to buy your groceries, and when night time comes they'd want you to come out of Merlin. I tried my exams for high school up there at Merlin. My hair used to be braided. This is years ago. Joe Shadd, Eileen's first husband, was trying his exams too. We were all there together. We weren't bothering these ones, and one of these boys he hollered, like he was up high on the stairs, and there was boys down on the ground, and he hollered down to him and asked him if he saw any "red-headed nigger." He called me a "red-headed nigger," and no sooner did he say "red-headed nigger," Joe Shadd just took his fist and hit him and knocked him down the stairs!

They had a big time over there. The news got to Buxton before we got here! Joe's teacher come down — she was here in Buxton too. Mr. Alexander and them had to go out to Merlin, to the school board out there. Mr. Alexander went out there and told them that all of us come from school: we weren't sent out there to fight; we were sent out there to go to school. I'm like Arlie. Arlie Robbins used to say, "June, you and I are the only ones believe that there's prejudice all around."[2] A lot of them got a sly way of hiding it, but it comes out; it comes out.

Arlie said that her mother used to sew for these two sisters down there; her mother made sheets and everything for them. When they'd come over to their house her mother would pass tea and cookies. Arlie said when she got to going to school in Chatham she'd meet them on the street they wouldn't even speak to you. No. Wouldn't want to be bothered. People were all like that around here. It made us angry, but you know you're that angry, and you couldn't start anything. Mr. Alexander, he didn't allow us to fight — and my mother and father didn't allow us to fight. So you just had to kind of take it.

They thought they were so much superior and how. There's a doctor in Chatham, a prominent doctor who's dead now, but his wife is still living. He was out in Merlin, and that's the way he made his money — when doctors used to come to your house, you know. He lived out there in Merlin and everybody went to him. Soon as he moved to Chatham, his wife went south. She had a great big dinner. Her boys had returned from the army. My sister and some more was working there. They come out and got a whole bunch of us girls. We all went there, and when we had gotten there, these little boys — they wouldn't be very old — she wanted us to call them master like they do down south — slavery. We all decided we're going to wait right till near supper time for them to sit down at the table. We all got up and walked out, just left.

There was a man come from a good home. His folks were well thought of. He got married; he wanted to buy a house on Victoria Avenue and they wouldn't let him. This doctor, he got the petition and he wouldn't let him buy on Victoria Avenue in Chatham. There was a great big write-up in the paper about that. That must've been in the 40s. Black people all lived in the east end. It's just in this last twenty or twenty-five years they let 'em buy property in different parts again. Now coloured people's all over Chatham. At one time you had to stay almost in your part of the town.

A lot of those white women thought: oh you coloured people. We could work for 'em, but they didn't want you up home on level with 'em. A lot of 'em felt they were so much smarter than coloured women. They're always trying to put our race down. It don't matter what vocation or what you're in, they're always trying to put you down.

When we first moved to Chatham two or three girls got a job in a store. But the funniest thing was, an ad came in the paper. Olive Steele, Eugene's sister, applied for a job at the Bell Telephone. When she applied for this job at the telephone — when she called — they said they had a opening. By the time she got over there, they said it was filled. She said while she was standing there, talking to a woman, another girl come in, and they hired this girl for the job because they didn't want coloured. I said, "Who was the boss over there?" When she told me the girl's name I said, "I used to work for her mother."

A few women worked in the store. They were clerks, but you couldn't hardly tell them from whites. They were from Dresden. Most of the coloured girls were on the elevators, and you'd get tired of that and move on to something different. They had it hard in Chatham, but Chatham's just like any other city.

I never got married. I worked all the time. My mother was crippled, so my brother and I decided we weren't going to get married; we would stay and take care of my mother. Then she had a heart attack, and him and I worked. We paid a lady to stay with my mother. But before my mother got real bad, Reverend Brown and them would have bus trips. I used to buy my mother a new outfit, take her on that. We'd go off: we went to Buffalo; we went to New York, Chicago. We'd go on those buses.

But you could never do too much for your mother. A lot of children's got mothers and they threw 'em off. I used to say, "Oh, if I could only just bring my mother back," 'cause I think children, you love your father and everything too, but there's nothing like ma.

We moved back to Buxton from Chatham about fourteen years ago. We moved back after my brother got through working on the railroad. I told him let's build a house out in Buxton because I couldn't drink the water in Chatham.

Now and then I help out with the museum. If I have something I think they would need or want, I'll offer it to the museum. After I come out here for a while, I used to help them over here at the church.

I'd tell young women to work 'cause work ain't gonna hurt you; work is good for you. Back in the olden days, people walked — they didn't ride — people walked, and all the women, they'd make cakes from scratch and everything.

Working don't hurt you; it's good for you. I've been working all these years. If it wasn't for having a little arthritis in my hands. I got scalded when I was thirty-seven — I got both legs scalded and my feet were scalded. If it wasn't for my feet being scalded, I'd feel just like I was when I was seventeen!

Notes

1. Many Chatham and Buxton Blacks have numerous relatives in Ohio, Kentucky and the South. Many Blacks who were fugitives from slavery and had settled in southwestern Ontario returned to the U.S. after Emancipation was proclaimed in the U.S. in 1867.

2. Arlie Robbins wrote and self-published *Legacy to Buxton*, a book about the Black settlement there.

Gwen Johnston
1915

From what little we know, my grandmother's mother came from Maryland. I hesitate to say via the Underground Railroad. I don't know exactly how they did get here — that's the problem; I'm not exactly certain. You know the old people often didn't tell you very much, for one reason or another. I always assumed they were free, but they may not have been.

Now my grandmother, Rosetta Amos — when she got married, Rosetta Amos Richardson — was born here. She was born in 1857 in Toronto. I have a picture of her where she was ninety-six and in very good health; it wasn't until just about the end of her life that she started to go down, but she died of old age. There wasn't anything really wrong with her. She was in her own home because of the wonderful care that her daughters gave her: she was in her own home and she died in her own bed. I think that that's really valuable because so many people don't have that privilege.

Her mother might have been nineteen or so when she had her. Grandma was married at seventeen and then started to have children right along.

My grandmother didn't talk too much about the early life, but she talked a little later on about her life as a married woman and as a mother. She talked about the little house that she bought on Lippincott Street and how Bathurst Street was just a cow pasture in those days. To earn a living grandma did sewing, she did all kinds of baking, and she did washing.

The Black community was small but very close-knit. Our churches were the British Methodist Episcopal Church on Chestnut Street, then there was First Baptist Church at University and Edward, and then Grant AME on Soho Street. Now those were the three churches, and our social life and spiritual life and everything revolved around those three churches — everybody knew everyone.

My mother tells us the story of how when she was quite young they had to deliver the laundry. There was some wealthy people living on Brunswick Avenue and on Huron Street and those streets, and Grandma would do the washing. My mother and her youngest brother would have to deliver the washing back to these people.

My mother was the youngest daughter of that family. There was seven because one brother — Arthur, his name was — he went to live in New York at a very early age, and the other brother, Sam, went to live in Montreal — they both lived away from Toronto for the remainder of their lives.

There was also Aunt Edith; she was the oldest daughter and she married a Jackson later on. And my other aunt, Mrs. Bessie Fountain, lived in London, raised her family in London.

My mother's name was Harriet Nelson. The women in the family did mainly domestic work. My Aunt Edith was a very excellent cook and she had cooking jobs, but they did domestic work — there was no other work that Black people could get in those days. The brother that went to New York worked on the trains, and the one known as Uncle Sam, who moved to Montreal, I don't know what he did — I think he worked on trains for a while too. Then Uncle Ernest — he worked in his early years; he worked in the post office, and then he went into the ministry, and he was one of the British Methodist Episcopal ministers.

In those days, the minister would be assigned. First of all, the British Methodist church had a connection of churches all over Ontario and they would have a conference once a year or so. They had the conferences every year and then they would move them.

The minister would perhaps be assigned to Owen Sound for a few years, and then he would be changed to Niagara Falls, or St. Catharines, or wherever the churches were. The reason for that was some of the congregations and the ministries were better than others, and they gave them a chance to perhaps make a slightly better living. It was very hard, but it was also very beautiful. At the conference you would get to meet everyone.

A lot of the churches have fallen away now, but all of that property belonged to the British Methodist Episcopal congregation, and the people in those cities, they bought and maintained those churches from the sweat of their brow, and they were very proud of it.

My grandmother was a very religious woman and active in the missionary society. It still is in operation. I think that in the early days they were organized to help people in other lands, but now I'm not so sure how much of that they do.

The stewards and the stewardesses sort of looked after old age, but the stewardesses they looked after the money side; they were the custodians and any of the social things that the church might be doing.

The lay preachers they would take over for the minister if he wasn't able to be there, and they sort of supported him in all the work that he did, went with him to funerals and sometimes weddings. Definitely, definitely the church was the focal point of the community in those days.

We all lived in Grandma's house on Lippincott Street. She was a very strong person, really tough. I mean she didn't let anybody get away with anything. I loved to go to dances and so on, and, of course, being so religious, she didn't agree with that at all. Had it not been for my mother, I wouldn't have had much social life. And theatre — you couldn't even go to a theatre. This was my grandmother's way, but we would sneak off and go sometimes and enjoyed it. She was very disciplinarian, but she did teach us to the best of her ability how to live your life and taught us many wonderful things about keeping house and cooking and sewing, knitting — all of those things.

She was an ambitious woman, and she felt that Black people should be able to do things like have a restaurant, so she worked hard and she did that — had a restaurant. She was a great person also for buying property. She bought quite a bit of property in the early days; if she was a young woman now, she'd know what to do with it! She was like the young women that we have now that are coming along that are just wonderful — that are into all sorts of things, and they have the opportunity to do many wonderful things — she was that kind of woman.

My grandfather was sort of a quiet man. He loved his family very much, but he didn't have his wife's ambition. He worked at the University of Toronto as sort of a custodian and he was the other side of the family. Of course, the daughters could always go and cry on Grandpa's shoulder if they had any problems. He died very early on. I was ten months old when he died — I was born in 1915, so I didn't know him at all, but my mother often talked about him. She loved him very much, but I didn't know him.

His name was Richardson — Samuel Cromwell Richardson — and his people came up to St. Catharines. I don't really know anything about them except that they came from Virginia — Grandma's people came from Maryland and Grandpa's people came from Virginia.

Growing up here, I was very protected. We had a big family and the family was all around us; members of the family would go away perhaps — Uncle Frank to his family to New York state and St. Catharines, but they always came back home. Grandma always kept that home so that any of the family who needed it they could come.

My mother was a very good, kind woman. She was the youngest daughter. Oh, she was wonderful! She was so giving: if there was anything I wanted, she tried to get it for me; she would do without so I could have something. She just had me — I had a lot of protection from all of them.

It's not that much that I can really tell about my mother. She worked very hard, but I had a wonderful childhood because of her. She was about twenty-two when she had me, but it was hard for her. My dad hadn't done his share at all, he had deserted us, and she had to struggle along. She never really got over that. My mother was a really sort of tender person, and she never really got over that, but she had her mother and her sisters to lean on, and they were wonderful.

Later, she took a very severe stroke and she suffered a lot. She lingered on in that condition for a long time. Better you go right away if you have a stroke or a heart attack — if you linger on it's worse than hell.

My Auntie Edith, she lived to be as old as Grandma. She was a very strong person; she held up the family. Then Aunt Bessie, she married and lived in London and had four children; the youngest daughter she lost early; her one son died just a few weeks ago. Two daughters are still living.

I went to school when I was seven. I'll never forget the day I went — scared to death. Hated it. I went to King Edward School — it's still standing, that was my primary school — and it's on Lippincott, just north of College near Bathurst Street. Then when I went to high school; I went to Central Technical School which is just up, so there was no excuse for being late, but often you managed to be.

In school I was very much alone, very much alone. Often I was the only Black child in my class. Sometimes there'd be maybe two, three of us at the most in the whole school.

I wouldn't say a lot of Black people lived on Lippincott. The Sharpe family was living north of Harbord Street, but the Sharpes didn't go to King Edward School; they were in a different district.

Going to school in the '20s was enjoyable in many ways. It was a Jewish neighbourhood then and you had your Jewish friends. When you grow up in a community where there are many white people, you don't really miss your own people, except on the weekends where you would see them at church and so on. If you didn't see them, then you would really be upset. But you got along. If you were a friendly person, you got along. Of course, sometimes there was some name-calling, but if there was any name-calling, either my grandmother or my mother would go straight to their parents.

I must say I didn't enjoy Central Tech that much. I was always getting lost in the halls. It was so big — and to find your room you had to be there at a certain time. I only stayed a couple of years, and then I got out into the work force.

I got out to work because it was becoming necessary financially, and, I guess, I was pretty sick of school. I went out into the work force, which was a mistake because by then you really haven't got an education, but I started out in the same way, working in private families — I was sixteen or so — and did that until I married.

I was twenty-two when I got married, so it was quite a few years that I was working. You get married because you fall in love with someone, for one thing. Years ago this was the thing to do: when you grew up you got married, you made a home. Thinking of Leonard, we really knew each other from the time we were children, from very young. He sort of lived in the west end of Toronto — farther west in the Italian area. We knew each other as children, and then we didn't see each other for a long time 'cause his people weren't people to come to church — his mother was Anglican. I met him when we all became teenagers and in our early twenties; we all got together Sunday evenings going to the Baptist church or going to the different things that the BME Church had, the dances and whatever. That's how people met. He was always very kind; he was full of life, full of jokes. That's what I liked about him. Very, very kind and honest. I liked his honesty. Lennie is very fair. Whatever it is, he is a fair person, and so we got along very nicely on that level.

When we got married — this was '38, '39 — life was hard. There was no work; we went through the Depression. Everybody in our family cooperated: whatever they earned sort of all went into the pool and to keep things going. Black people were wonderful to each other during the Depression. I don't think that Black people suffered — some suffered more than others — but they shared what they had and they got through. We can always laugh and we can always have a social time.

As far as clothing and different things like that went, people worked for people with money, and they would always hand down clothes, and you fix them up — this is how you kept yourself dressed. The Depression was hard, but I don't think it was as hard for Black people as it was for white people because we were closer knit. We were used to doing without.

I think this is very important: how earlier on, even during the days of the Depression, Black people could not get an apartment in a decent area, and that lasted long after the Depression. Young Black women could not get into a hospital to train as a nurse. Whenever anyone asks me what it was like years ago, I always draw this example because I think it's important that they understand exactly what it was like. It wasn't until several years later when people fought very hard to make changes, like the Don Moores.

I was born at home, in a little room upstairs on Lippincott Street. All Grandma's family had all of their children at home. They had a doctor, a Dr. Margaret McAlpen, and she was at the corner of Ulster and Bathurst. I'll never forget her. She did the deliveries with Grandma sort of helping. They always had a doctor, but everybody was born at home, didn't go to the hospital — people generally Black or white didn't go to hospitals; they liked to be at home.

After Lennie and I married, I didn't work. He preferred

that I stay at home, and it wasn't easy because he worked on the trains and the wages were very small, but we went along — we managed with what we had.

We lived for a very short time with Leonard's parents, and we lived in Grandma's house for a very short time. Then we moved. When Leonard got work just outside Galt I went up. Of course, I took all our stuff and I went up to be with him. I wasn't going to be here and my husband there. He was so surprised and so pleased when I came. He said, "Gwenny, I didn't think you'd come." I said, "Oh yes. We're married and I'm here."

He was already there working on the machine job and we couldn't find a place to stay in Galt. Some people in Galt said there's a Black man — Ira Johnston was his name — who lives just up the road in Preston. So we went up, knocked on his door, and he said, "I was just looking for a young couple to come and help keep house here." So we stayed there. Lennie had a long way to go back every day to work in Galt, but Mr. Johnston was very kind — he was beautiful old man. We stayed there for a while, then we came back to Toronto. Then just before the war we went out and we got our own little place.

Then our daughter Carol was born. We were living on a street called Morningside, at Swansea; we had a little basement apartment at that time and we were there for five years. Then in that time Clayton was also born and we looked around for a house. We bought this house when Carol was four and Clayton wasn't quite two. That was in the '40s. It is an old house, but a very well-constructed one, so we've been here ever since.

Leonard had always talked about what things could be like for Black people, and as he puts it, finally he put his money where his mouth is. We saved and he decided to open a bookstore. First, he went and worked in a bookstore to learn how it goes, and then, in the beginning, he had a partner, but it didn't work out. I was working in a craft store, and he asked me if I would come in with him, so I quit there and then. At that time, we were on Walton Street — that was the first location. Walton is just south of Gerrard and off Bay.

We had this little store, which was a surprise to some of the book publishers. They said to Leonard that he'd never make any money on that street — it's off the beaten path — but Lennie's a great one to take a chance, so we opened that little store — and talk about having fun! All the different people who passed — that was the Black Power days and all kinds of people came from the States. That was '68. It was very interesting — we had a wonderful time; it's nothing like that now.

I remember my daughter — my youngest daughter, Christine. We had talked about going natural, and this particular night she came home and she said, "Come, Mom," and she washed my hair, and she said, "You're on your own." I was a little nervous going to work the next day, but I carried my head very high, and my boss looked at me and she said, "Well, I like it better the other way," and I said, "This is me. This is the way I'm gonna stay."

Then we outgrew that location and moved on to Bay Street.

When we were preparing to move to Bay Street I was frightened. I thought: how will I manage when Leonard is on the road? Because he stayed on the train so that we wouldn't have to take our living out of the store. Whatever came into the store could be ploughed back into the business. How we managed that was when he'd go — he was running out to Winnipeg — he'd call me when he got to

Sudbury, and if there were any problems we'd straighten it out, and when he got to Winnipeg the same, and the same back, so we managed all right.

But when we were moving to Bay Street the store was so much larger I thought: how would I manage? But I got used to it in a very short time — it's funny how you do. It was old hat after the first few days and I was quite comfortable there. We enjoyed Bay Street. Running a business, and especially this kind of business, a specialized Black bookstore, you have a lot of headaches. The money doesn't come into you like it comes to Coles or W.H. Smith — they've got a lot of money behind them. We don't, and we just have to keep building and sacrifice, but it's worth it.

It's worth it because we feel that we have been instrumental in our people learning about themselves. When we were children and sat in school there was nothing taught about the wonderful history of Africa, nothing about what Black people had contributed to the world — can you imagine? They just tried to cut us out of history, and so we feel that in a small way we've been able to open these doors.

People come from all over for information about our history, our heritage, so if nothing more we feel that it's worth it for that reason. And then all the beautiful friends we've met — young people who come around — and it's worth it. People have come and felt it's sort of an oasis in a cold place. A lot of people that came very young and have grown up with us — we feel as though they are our children.

When we were growing up, the UNIA was a wonderful place, sort of a second home for us, that's what the little building at 355 College Street was. Every Sunday afternoon there would be some kind of speeches; they had their meetings, and people gathered there and listened to the speaker and socialized — then when Marcus Garvey came, of course, that was a wonderful time in the hall.

When the UNIA started I was very young. I remember being taken there on Sunday afternoons, and I remember when Marcus Garvey came, and we children didn't know what he was talking about, but we were compelled to listen — just to sit there and be quiet and listen to him.

I only remember that when Marcus Garvey was here they had as usual the Sunday afternoon meeting. The hall was full of people and he was talking about his philosophy. Certainly, the UNIA brought Black people together. There were two factions here: there were the people who were members of the UNIA — back then it was called the UNIA — and then there were the people that sort of followed the Home Service Association, and also an awful lot of the church people didn't follow UNIA.[1]

The dances we used to have at the UNIA — they were fantastic! Every Thursday night, of course, at the hall there'd be a dance. Every Thursday night — that was the night that the domestics got off. It was wonderful because they would have chairs all around the hall, and parents would come to sort of see how their children were doing. The parents would act as chaperons, and they'd sit around if they didn't dance. They came and they sat there and enjoyed themselves watching the younger people dance.

It was very inexpensive to get in — that's fifty cents. Cyril McLean had a wonderful little orchestra — maybe four- or five-piece, and it was a good band — and he used to come and play there. He played piano, jazz piano, and Raymond Coker played saxophone. And there was a Roy Worrell — he played trumpet very good. It wasn't till later on that the disco starts coming in, but we had live music

— all kinds of jazz. It was wonderful. Every Thursday night. You never cared about Friday morning. It was such a good time; it was dancing and meeting friends, and romance bloomed from there.

It was either at the hall that you met people or at the church. There was a period when the First Baptist Church was just a meeting place. The young people would just be in crowds outside. This was when they were at University and Edward Street, the first location. There would just be crowds of young people out there. Some of the deacons from the church would come out and say, "Please young people come in and sit down." They didn't want to — they just wanted to talk and meet people, and that's what went on for a long, long time. It was gorgeous! Really, really wonderful!

There was an organization — a club, the Dunbar Literary Society. That was in the '30s — that was before I was married — and they would have their Dunbar Ball. Now this was a formal thing. They had their dances — not every year — but I'm telling you, you never saw such gowns and tails and top hats. It was marvellous!

I'm not sure who founded the Dunbar Literary Society, but I know that the ball was fantastic![2] And they also had club meetings and different things. It's too bad that Grace Trotman isn't with us any longer because she kept her finger on all that sort of thing.

Mme. Leona Brewton was instrumental in putting on all of these wonderful literary things. I used to recite Paul Laurence Dunbar's poetry from time to time when we had different affairs, like *In the Morning: 'Lias! Lias! Bless de Lawd! | Don' you know de day's erbroad? | Ef you don't git up, you scamp, | Dey'll be trouble in dis camp.*

Of course, she would insist that you take part, get up

there and say your piece, or play the piano, or do whatever you could do, or sing. She was just marvellous that way; she brought a lot of people out that way who would be shy and standing back.

We don't do recitations — we should. We want to be entertained all the time. The only thing we have now is television — isn't it a shame!

I don't get to church too often now. Once in a while I go to First Baptist. I'm ashamed to say I don't got to my home church, the BME, very often, but First Baptist is very lively. It's lovely to go there on a Sunday morning, or on special occasions — it's nice anytime. You have to get there early, or you won't even get a seat; people really come and you come away feeling good. Go once in a while; you don't have to go all of the time — I don't believe in being there all the time. I moved on from that, but I do enjoy going once in a while. Junie and I will say to each other, "Let's go to church Sunday morning," — special occasions like Christmas, Easter, times like that, — and we always come away feeling good, glad that we went.

I guess I'd have to say June is my best friend. She is a very, very good friend. I've known Junie and Danny forty-nine years.[3] I met Junie before I got married. June came to Toronto — I don't know just what year she came to Toronto — but I met her, I think at the church — and Danny, of course, I knew his family. I didn't know him well then, but I knew his family because they lived on Lippincott Street. They lived down closer to College, and so I knew Danny and Edna, his sister.

I think as far as Black people are concerned we have to get closer to our men, work out our problems; don't let women's liberation separate us because that would be a disaster. Black women have in some ways always been liberated. We've had to be. We've had to go out there and help our men bring in the bread, and if there wasn't a man we'd have to bring in the bread on our own. I think that we have to be very, very careful about getting separated from the Black men. Black men and Black women have to get closer together, work out their problems, and sometimes women's liberation gets in the way — women's liberation as defined by white women.

Black men and Black women most certainly have to work out respect and regard for each other. A lot of Black young people come into Third World Book and Crafts and talk. Young Black men talk about they can't find a Black woman to be friends or associate with, or fall in love with, or marry eventually. Now I'm not always sure that they are telling the truth, or they understand what it is they're saying. Their main complaint usually is that if they go out with a Black woman, it is how much money it is they have to spend that she cares about. She wouldn't share the evening, perhaps. I don't say on the first date you should say, "I'll pay half," but as you go along share it — because nine times out of ten, she's earning more money than he is as things stand today.

When I was coming along, the young man had to have enough money to pay for everything on an evening — he wasn't much if he couldn't; you weren't much if you paid. But that has all changed, thank goodness, because how can you do that? Especially today when things are so expensive. And it's just not fair anyway. Pay part; sometimes take him out.

But a lot of the young men complain to me; they come and cry on my shoulder; they say that they can't find a Black woman who is interested. Either it's money or his skin is too Black; he's not this, he's not that. The women come and complain that they can't find a Black man because the Black men are all going with the white women. So we have to work all this out. We have to learn to love ourselves; let us get together and be a nation, because if we don't, we'll be forever enslaved, forever at the bottom of the heap. Look at it economically, look at all the money we spend for everything, and none of it stays in our community. It all goes right out. We give all back and this is a disaster. What we must do as a race is learn respect for each other, sit down together and work out our problems, be honest with each other, so that we'll get the fruits of our labour. It should be that we wake up and work on our economic condition.

Notes

1. Some opposition to Garveyism went along nationalist lines — West Indians vs. Canadian-born Blacks. Also, Garvey's idea of Canada as merely a place of sojourn for Blacks, their ultimate destination being Africa, met with resistance from some Canadian Blacks. See Winks, *op. cit.*, p. 416. Today the organisation is called the UAIA.

2. The Dunbar Literary Society was named for the early African-American poet Paul Laurence Dunbar. According to Winks, these clubs lapsed in the 1920s, but Gwen Johnston's recollection indicates the club continued into the 1930s. Dunbar Literary Societies were found in both Canada and the United States.

3. June and Danny Braithwaite.

Grace Fowler
1919

I'm from Winnipeg and got married to a Chatham Township fellow and moved up here in '44. You got to live here a hundred and fifty years before you're a Buxtonite (laughter). And you've got to marry into the Shreves, Shadds, or Princes, or you haven't got it made (laughter).

I married a Fowler from Chatham Township — we always referred to him as a "Chatham Township hillbilly." He had the old-fashioned ideas about women being in the home and all that, but I was an enlightened woman, even back then. I was almost twenty-five when I got married. That was what I told him: "You should have married a fifteen-year-old and raised her the way you wanted her." But we stayed married for twenty-seven years, raised four kids.

We started out with twenty acres, and then the 401 come along; we sold that, and we bought a hundred acres farther down the road. I did most of the farming because he was a railroad man. Like when you were out on the tractor, planting the beans or whatever, you had the kids in little orange boxes, or riding on the tractor with you — you just did it. And when my husband was away I looked after the animals — we had a cow, and we raised pigs — so I fed them and cleaned the stalls. See, I didn't work out anywhere. For my money I had a big garden, and I used to can all my vegetables and fruits; I'd can anywhere from about three to five hundred quarts of fruits and vegetables.

It was damn hard work. We didn't have fridges and freezers in them days; we had iceboxes, so you had to can meat and everything. It kept you busy. And I used to sew all my kids' clothes. And tomato picking time, I'd go out and pick tomatoes — that was for my cash. That bought the materials to make my kids' clothes and bought their school books when they were going to school. My husband was a railroad man, and at that time he was making eighty dollars a month. Tips were good, but that was all the wages were.

We bought twenty-five acres down there on the ninth concession, and we were planting soy beans, and I was riding the drill. All of a sudden, here come this great big snake up over. Well, I got off there — I jumped off there and went running — beat that tractor, and I screamed, and my husband stopped, and he went back and killed it. It had to be at least five feet long. Newspaper came out, took pictures of it. It scared the devil out of me.

I would go to somebody else's farm and pick tomatoes, and then I used to grow cucumbers as a cash crop — darn lot of work to that. That's a seven-day-a-week job. You don't stop for the Sabbath or anything; you just go out there and pick cucumbers until you're cross-eyed.

We started out with twenty-five acres and then down the road had a hundred acres. Now my husband and I are separated — and I've got fifty acres and he's got the other fifty. Edwin Shadd sharecrops my fifty, and all I do is pick up the cheque — and then I give it to the government!

Mostly we planted corn, soya beans, wheat. We tried tomatoes one year, but they didn't turn out as well as they might've. That was down on the twenty-five acres. And then it was a lot of work because I had to do most of the work when my husband was away. Tomatoes is a cash crop, but with the cost of the spraying and the plants and everything, we didn't really make that much that year, so we never tried it again. And most of the year we had corn and soya beans.

After we got on the hundred acres we used to hire someone to take the crop off, but when we were down on the twenty-five acres we didn't even have machinery; we used to borrow my husband's Uncle Tom's tractor, and then we'd go from daylight till we got done at night time. I remember the first year that it happened: I was driving the tractor, he was driving the cultivator. We were doing the beans, and every time I closed my eyes, all I could see was beans coming at me. It was awful because we was on that tractor — started at daybreak and worked right on with the lights on at night until we got done it, ten or eleven o'clock at night, and the kids were all on this tractor, they were crying, and they were tired, and they wanted to go.

As to how I managed having the kids with me — that's why I say my husband was a hillbilly. That was women's work: he didn't look after the kids. When we came in I'd been riding the tractor all day, but I fixed the supper, I washed the dishes, I got the kids ready for bed. He lay down on the couch and went to sleep because he thought it was women's work, and then he didn't do women's work. I'm not supposed to be tired. That's my whole life too, around him. Just the fact that he was around should have given me enough energy!

I was born and raised in Winnipeg. My mother's from

England; my dad was from Kansas City, Missouri. In Winnipeg a young Black girl wouldn't have had too much of a problem if she stayed like with other Black people — not that they had that many Black people, but they did have places they congregated. But when you were mixed blood like me, nobody wanted you: whites didn't want you and Blacks didn't want you.

I was never around coloured people until I was about seventeen and I had gone to work in Winnipeg. My mother lived outside of Winnipeg — she had moved there. In 1932 we had moved out to the country, where the government had a back-to-the-land movement. She bought ten acres of rock out there, and that's when I got to like the country and got used to the country because I used to work for farmers. Call it work — didn't get much for it: you'd get seventy-five cents a day for loading sheaves and taking them to the tractor.

When I was fourteen — I was fourteen in December, and in January I got a job working for this man. I was working for board and room and clothes. They fed me real good. And I did everything: I fed horses, curried horses, slopped hogs, milked cows, cleaned barns, cut wood, I worked in the house — I was a farm help, and because I was a girl I did both jobs. And they had four boys who didn't talk a word of English — I had to learn German so I could talk to them, and eventually they learned English from talking to me.

I just got room and board and my clothes, and my clothes amounted to a pair of gum rubber boots that the man had re-soled, and his wife gave me one of her dresses — now at the time I weighed about eighty-five pounds and she weighed a hundred and sixty! So I took the dress home, and my mother made a dress and a skirt out of it for me.

My mother came down there. It was spring and I was working out in the field. Then you didn't have tractors: you had horses, you didn't ride on anything, you walked behind the plough, you walked behind everything. I was working out in the field just like a man, so she told this fellow that I was working for that she thought I should get a wage. He paid me five dollars a month, but I didn't get it in cash.

In the fall, I took home potatoes and a butchered hog and all sorts of stuff for my mother 'cause she was out there alone. She had seven kids — I'm the middle one — and there was still a few kids at home. That first year I didn't see any cash.

This is back in the Depression time. Kids don't really know. I know. I remember my mother worrying about so many things — not that she wasn't a worrier, but with kids everything's fun, it don't matter. But things were tight. You could buy eggs for five cents a dozen. I saw the farmer I worked for take his piglets to market — his six week old pigs — and couldn't sell 'em and dropped 'em in the river in a bag when he came back because he couldn't afford to feed 'em. I took a piglet home to my mother — that was part of my wages — and she raised that pig, and I don't know how many litters she raised from it.

She called her Rusty. It was one of those red Thamesworth. I remember when Rusty got too old to keep around anymore. She used to follow my mother around like a dog. She went down to the village for mail, the pig went with her. And so she had to sell it, and the buyer couldn't get in because the road was muddy, so my mother had to take Rusty up to the road, and she came home just crying, saying, "I feel like Judas."

Then I worked for a dairy farmer in Beausejour. That

was just a case of milking cows all the time, it seemed like. I worked as a hired girl, indoors and out. He had about forty cows that we had to milk morning and night. I remember I got a calf from him for fifty cents and took it home. It was one of the best cows my mother ever had.

In Manitoba you have to go to school until you're fourteen. I didn't like those kids out there at all. They'd never seen any Black person before, and I had to be punching somebody in the mouth everyday, so I told my mother, when I was fourteen, I'm quitting school, and I went and got a job. The next job I had paid three dollars a month; the other, seventy-five cents.

That three dollars I got bought me a hat, a dress, a pair of shoes, stockings and left me enough for my bus ride to go home and visit my mother.

When I was seventeen or eighteen I went to Winnipeg and I got a job as a maid — worked for these Scotch people. Lovely. A lady and she had three sons. They were grown men, but they were very nice people. I can't remember what my wages were — nothing to write home about — fourteen dollars a week, something like that.

I was the first Black girl that sold her colour to try and join the army in Winnipeg. They gave me a hard time. I was going to drop it, but there was a Mrs. Brown who had a Black Girl Guide troop and she said, "Go on, Grace. Keep trying. Some other girl will come on after you and she'll want it. And if you change the way, then she won't have those problems."

So I went right on through, until they called me for the physical. They tried to make out like their basic concern was would I get along. One Black girl with all these white people?! I'd been getting along with them all my life. Why should it change? So they kept calling me back and asking me more questions and filling out more forms, and I'm getting really pissed off. But I told Mrs. Brown that I'd carry through.

There was a recruiting officer there — she was very nice, very understanding. The day they called me I asked about her and she had gone out with a group to train. If I could've gone with her, I still might have joined the army, but she was gone. So they called me in to get my physical, and I told them, "When I want one I'll go to my own doctor!" and I hung up on them. By then I was absolutely disgusted.

I think it must have taken about three months, and I told them, "I'm not asking you for something, I'm offering it to you. And you're giving me a hard time trying to give it to you."

So I got over it. By then I'd met my husband, so I didn't give a damn whether I joined the army or not. He was what we called in Winnipeg the "floating population" — that was the CPR porters — because they were in and out. There was a restaurant there it was run by Black people; it was called the Rumble G Inn and I met him there.

That's where I met our lieutenant governor, Lincoln Alexander, too. He was in the air force and I was working at the Rumble G Inn; he used to come there for breakfast — more or less for company with your own.

It's hard to say what my husband was like because of the fact that we separated, but he was a very nice-looking man. He's three years older than me, and he had some weird ideas, but when you're in love you don't think about all these weird ideas — they work out afterwards. He was a good worker, and he had good weight on him, business-wise. When we got married in '44 we came to Toronto. I lived in Toronto for about a year.

He had the idea that when we got married I shouldn't work. We had one room and the use of the kitchen, and I was going stir crazy. Nothing to do all day. You'd go out and window shop, but then you'd spend money. So finally — that was the first time I'd bucked him — I went out and got a job, a job in a war plant. I worked on what they call the high explosives side, where you got paid a little extra because you were working with dangerous powders. We made detonators for torpedoes, and it wasn't a bad job. I learned every job on the line because it was awful boring just to stay in one. Some of the women stayed in one job all the time they were there, but I made the rounds — learned them all — and I liked every shift excepting the night shift.

When I worked in that war plant — especially on the night shift, when all the machinery breaks down — we used to get into some real good discussions. This one night we talked about nursing, and I was saying how they wouldn't let Black girls go into nursing at that time — and this supervisor was trying to explain to me why they didn't and was trying to be delicate about it. She was saying, "Well, you know your people have a different odour and somebody sick, they don't want somebody around them."

I said to her, "How many Black people are working in this shop right now?"

And she said, "Well, you're the only one."

I said, "I work alongside of some of these women. If I smelled as bad as them, I'd shoot myself, so don't talk to me about bad smell because you've got it here, and you don't have a Black person in it." So that stopped that conversation!

But it's true they get these weird ideas about things. I wasn't in a good mood anyhow because my husband and me had been trying to find a place to live. You talk to them on the phone: "Oh yes, a lovely place." One time there was one place we were going to — and we weren't sure we were going to the right place — so we stopped at the drug store on the corner and phoned, and we told him where we were. He said "Well, you're just a couple of doors away from where you are," and "No, the place hasn't been rented." We went up and knocked on the door. And the man took one look at us and slammed the door and said, "Sorry, it's rented."

Now we'd gone through this nearly all day, and I'm evil because Winnipeg was never as prejudiced as Toronto. Then I got on the streetcar to come home — and I'm tired and I'm hungry and I'm evil — and some dingbat in the back of the streetcar said, "That's the first time I saw a nigger with freckles." I wanted to kill somebody, but my husband there said, "Just ignore him, he don't know any better."

And at the next stop the back emptied, all these embarrassed white people got off. Then I come into work, and this woman started this stuff, and now, you know, that was the straw that broke the camel's back. I swear it was. I'm not saying that there wasn't prejudice in Winnipeg, but all the jobs I ever applied for, Charles was the only place — and that was the pancake house — that didn't hire Black people.

When I came to Toronto I was living at Mrs. Doderidge's place, and her and I were going out looking for a job. I know that woman was a nervous wreck when we got home because we rode for hours, it seemed like, on the streetcar and got out at some kind of factory — I don't know what it was. We went in, and as we were walking up to where you have to fill out the application, I saw this man walk over and say something to the woman. She said, "I'm sorry, we're not taking any more applications today." So I won't argue with that, that's their privilege, but when we went out I said to Mrs. Doderidge, "Let's just wait here for a minute." And there was two white girls walked in behind us and went up to the desk and started filling out applications.

I said, "Let's go on back."

Mrs. Doderidge said, "Oh no, let's just leave it alone."

I said, "I don't care what you're doing, but I'm going back," and I said to the clerk, "Well, since you're reopening applications, I guess I'll fill out an application."

And the clerk said, "Uh oh, I'm sorry...."

I said, "Now they're filling out. If you don't hire Black why don't you put it in the paper? Why have us come half-way across the country trying to get a job?"

She said, "Oh, we have Chinese working here. We have Japanese."

I said, "You got any Black people working here? Why am I arguing with you? I saw that man come over here and speak to you. He hasn't got enough guts to face me himself, so he sends you, and you're only doing your job, so I won't argue any more, but I wish he had enough nerve to come over here and talk to me because I'd like to talk to him for a while."

But he didn't; he went out and shut the door. So then we went over to a place where they make chocolates and ran into the same thing. I'm mad by now and Mrs. Doderidge is trying to shush me up. I said, "For God's sake! If the colour came off, it isn't going to show on your damn chocolate." Boy, I was mad.

In some restaurants in Winnipeg they hired us, but most restaurants did not hire Blacks. Mr. Moore, the restaurant owner, he was an Englishman with some weird ideas. The funny part was most restaurants were three-storey. The second floor of this restaurant was a private club, and the waitress on our floor was Black because club members wanted a Black waitress. When the private Kinsmen came in for their luncheons they wanted a Black girl to wait on them. White girls got mad as hell because the Kinsmen used to give good tips, and they either used the private dining room or the mezzanine. We always waited on them because they asked for us — that was because we'd worked in service and we knew how to serve.

These white girls would come with armloads of plates and just sling them at them. We had worked in service where you were taught to serve properly, and that's what they wanted. I used to tell Mr. Moore — him and I used to sit down; I used to get out of a lot of work having discussions with him — "If the public is going to object, why do all these big shots ask for us?"

They had a dining room on the third floor, all Black waitresses. That was a public dining room; it was more high-class than down on the first floor, and it cost you more to go up there, so this is all high-class white people. There was the Kinsmen, the Lions Club, the Oddfellows: they all used to come to the restaurant and hold their meeting there while they had their lunch, and they always asked for Black waitresses. Most private parties they wanted us. So I told them, "If we're good enough in there, why aren't we good enough out on the floor?" We were only bus girls on the main floor.

I got married in September, and I got a job at the war plant in November, I think it was. But I'm still not used to this humid Ontario weather. Out west it gets cold, but it's dry cold — I never wore woolly underwear or anything until I came up here. I'd be standing waiting for a streetcar and I'd been shivering to death. My husband thought I was sickly at first; in September I'd have a heavy coat on, and everyone else was walking around in a light coat. I'm cold and he can't understand it.

I used to go to big band dances at the Palais Royal, over the water. Lionel Hampton and Duke Ellington. Lionel Hampton's thing was to get his whole band marching around and to play that dah dah dah dah dah dah dah; everybody would jump and you could feel the floor shake. I said to Harold, "We're gonna go in the darn drink, and I haven't got a bathing suit on!"

There was white people there at the Palais Royal too; they liked it. Toronto has a big Black population, but when a big band would come to Winnipeg, it would be more white than Black because Winnipeg's Black population isn't that big and it's spread out — they don't just live in a district. Oh, those big bands were something else. They used to have music in those days; now they got noise.

You'd wear what you'd call party dresses to hear the big bands, but they weren't usually long dresses. Some people'd have long dresses; I never even got into long dresses until I got into the union, started going to these banquets and things.

Then when the trend started to go the other way, back to short dresses, I gave all my dresses to my daughter who's a Muslim. She wears long dresses and she just rearranged them. All my kids can cook and sew.

After we moved to the farm, we used to have fun, especially at supper time. When you harvested, your thrashing crew travelled from farm to farm; your neighbours would come to help you, and then you'd go and help your neighbours. The farmers' wives came to each place and they'd help with the cooking; they used to put a spread on at supper time that you wouldn't believe — they fed the thrashing crew three times a day, at breakfast, lunch and dinner — and then at ten o'clock and four o'clock, they'd bring coffee and cookies and whatever else. You had a good time doing things together, but if there was a neighbour's wife that wasn't a good cook, that would be the last place that they'd go to.

I don't really know if it was harder for Black farmers to get loans because until I was up here, I never knew Black farmers. We never had any problems getting a loan. I don't think any farmers I know have a problem getting a loan. Nobody does — the bank is glad to give you a loan.

When I worked at the hospital there was this chef; he says, "All these darn farmers, they're making all this big money and it's costing us."

I said, "I don't know where you get that dumb idea. What you pay for a quart milk, that's what farmers get paid for a gallon."

He said, "How can they have all that big machinery and drive them big cars?"

I told him, "The bank lets them. That's the only reason because most of your stuff is in hock."

We didn't need any loan to buy our second property because we'd had a place — twenty-five acres down on the ninth — and then the 401 bought up our place. We got a better price because I opened my mouth again. My husband said, "You've got to take what they give you. Otherwise they take it off you." But I told the guy off — he was being so condescending, like you're lucky we're giving this to you.

I said, "You're just paying for the land. The fact is that I've got to move, I've got to make new neighbours, my kids have got to go to a different school. You're not involved at all, so don't come up here with all your condescending and telling me that I'm lucky to be getting this. You can tell me that you can come in here and take my farm away from me, but you might have a few bullet holes in you before you do because I'll shoot you." You can talk to me, you can argue with me, but don't be condescending with me.

We really only farmed a couple of years, and then my husband rented it out because I told him I'm not working out here like a slave anymore: if he wanted to stay home and look after it, fine. Like we used to keep about six sows: I would be there when they farrowed; I'd clean their pens out — and pigs don't smell sweet. You have to be careful with pigs because if a sow is in pain, she'll eat her pigs as fast as they're born. I'd be right there looking after them: I'd be cleaning out the pens; I fed them all the time — even when my husband was home and sometimes he'd be in town.

But when he sold the little pigs, he didn't even offer me a chocolate bar and say, "You did a good job, Gracie. Here's a chocolate bar." So that's when I told him, "You can get rid of those pigs because I'm not looking after them anymore."

He didn't believe me. One time he came home after a trip, and the sow was walking out of the pen because the manure got so deep that she could walk over the fence. She was out eating his crops.

He said, "What about the little pigs?" I said, "That's tough, I'm not doing it anymore." I wouldn't let them starve — I wouldn't let any animal starve — but I wasn't cleaning the pens.

So he sold them. And that's when he started renting out the farm. I told him I'm not going to be a workhorse and slug my brains out and I never get any compensation for it at all.

He said, "You live here."

I said, "I pay awful high rates for living here."

I believe in pay for equal work — however it's worded. But as far as a man can open the door for me, he can buy my dinner, he can buy my drinks. I'm not to the point where I want to do everything for myself. I do believe if you're doing a job of equal value then you should receive the pay. There is no way that a bank teller at this window is a man, and he's getting half again as the bank teller at this window, and *she's* more likely doing better job than him in the first place. So I do believe that women in the work field should be paid according to what their work is and not to be paid less because they're women.

I used that same argument at the hospital when they used to give us our raises by percentage. I don't hold with that because if it's five percent, the men at a higher wage is getting a higher rate, and the men that needs the raise isn't getting it. But when that guy with the higher wage is going in the store he's paying the same for his food. They don't say that because you're not getting the same money, you can get your bread and milk cheaper. So they finally went to a dollar-for-dollar deal.

I always fight for the underdog, and I think that started because I was the only scrapper in our family outside of my brother Harold. If somebody was pushing my brothers or sisters around, then I would take up for them — and I've been doing that for the rest of my life. And that's, I guess, why I was in the union. I was steward, chief steward, fighting for people so that they got their rights. But I fought for everybody but myself, which was ridiculous —

not that anybody ever took advantage of me, not more than once!

I was involved with the union right from the start. It was the Service Employees International Union, Local 210. Their office was in Windsor, and they came down to organize us, and I was right in on the organizing from the beginning. I can remember Mr. Pearce — he was administrator at the hospital. By then a law had been passed that you couldn't stop people from organizing, and they were getting ready to build a new wing. So he called a meeting to show us all what the new wing was gonna look like. Ordinarily, he'd never do this: they don't care if we knew what it looked like or not. And then after he got us into the meeting he started quoting prices — wages, what an organized hospital is getting, and what he was paying. So one of the fellows that was on the organizing with them reported this to the organizer, and the organizer went to their lawyer and told them, "If you don't want that man in jail, you better tell him to stop." So we didn't get any more of that.

We were organized in '67; we got our first contract in '68. I think it was in '72 I became chief steward. They sent me to their seminars — they used to have a seminar every year up near Lake Couchiching — and I went to that for five years. I took all the courses right from steward's training, collective bargaining, how to run a meeting, teach. I was chief steward when I retired in '84.

I believe that a woman can have a career and raise a family. A lot of people don't think so. But I do believe, if they possibly can during their younger years, it's nice if a woman can stay home. The kids get to know who they belong to. When they have baby-sitters — it's all right if you can hire, say, a housekeeper that stays right there, but when they have different baby-sitters they get so they don't really know who they belong to.

I belonged to this Recess Club, and that's what it was: a recess from your kids once a month. They started that back in 1942, I think. Ivy Brown is the only original member left. I came into it afterwards, but Arlie Robbins and Laverne used to belong to it. They met once a month at one of the couple's houses. You played cards, or you sat and gossiped, or whatever, and then they served lunch at midnight and that was it. That was a social evening. I used to get so teed off because I used to love playing cards.

I won't play any game that involves money. I won't gamble, and it's not because of my religion: it's just because I work so hard for my money, if somebody could get it from me like that, I'd kill 'em.

The men would all gather at the table right away and then the women would be left there. That's fine, I've got nothing against women. There they'd be sitting — we had a school teacher, one of our members, she'd be sitting there talking about all the cute things the kids did in school and the mothers be talking about all the cute things that the kids did at home — and I'm saying, "It's your play, spades are trump."

Finally I said, "My God, do you have to talk about your kids?"

They said, "Don't you love your kids?"

And I said, "Sure, but I can forget them once in a while too!"

So after that, as soon as the men got up and made a beeline I got up and made one with them — because men play cards, they just sit down there. But oh Lord, the women....

Esther Hayes
Eleanor Hayes

Esther H.:   If you're thinking of Negro history, children
             can't be taught it by white people because
             white people see history as the history of bat-
             tles — I'm not criticizing, it is a fact — land
             grabs and such things. Negro history is not the
             recording of battles. Negro history is al-
             together different: it is not written. Negro his-
             tory must be taught by Negroes, only by
             Negroes.

Eleanor H.: Negro history is being made now; Negro his-
             tory is current.

Esther H.:   One of the difficulties that we're having with
             our history is that we have too many people,
             too many different peoples that are included
             in Negro history. West Indian history, African
             history, Canadian Black history are absolutely
             different.

             I would think that in the community in
             Canada our history would start after the
             slaves came up here. It is more a history of
             trying to get recognition as people deserving

of equal opportunity. For instance, there was so much discrimination — real discrimination — and prejudice when my mother came to Canada and when I grew up as a child. I know the work we did in the community in order to get the white people to accept us — not accept us, recognize us.

What we went through in the past — that is history! That is history in Ontario, and that will include people who came over here from Africa or the West Indies. When I was a child I was taught Negro history, but it was more American Negro history — but at least it was a good basis. What I've got from studying Negro history is that I am equal to anybody: I am capable of doing it.

Today, I am very annoyed that we have not accomplished more than we have because we keep on going back to what we suffered. Let's move ahead. We're not moving ahead, and I believe that one reason is that the Black community is built on women, and they have never been accepted as the people equal to Black men. The women have always had a lesser part in consideration, but they have accomplished the most. The men have accomplished nothing, absolutely nothing.

When we were kids we used to go to the UNIA Hall, and you'd see the women up there. They're working as house cleaners, and they'd get their children all dressed up and bring them to the hall to sit down to learn something about their own community. You can see in those faces every mother hoping that her child would make it, but she has nothing to build on. All she has to build on is: "I've worked with the white people in the white people's houses, and they have a son the same age as my son, and their son is getting ahead. Why can't my son get ahead? If I take him to church, and I dress him well, he will get ahead." But that's not it. You don't build on that.

What's not there for us to build on is a recognition of my capability to recognize that I am equal to everyone else. Another thing is that I feel that these parents were always saying, "Don't do this to disturb the white man." When I say that I'm studying Negro history I say, "The white man did it, I can do it." That is a start.

There've been so many disappointments! The children couldn't get anyplace because the children didn't have the basics. All the mother had was hope — where the Black men were I don't know. In the Black community and the groups we had at the UNIA Hall, at first the men worked with the women — then at a certain age the young men disappeared, and the women were carrying on still.

Eleanor H.: I feel that enough emphasis has not been put on education. There is a recognition that there is a need for education, but there's no physical means. I used to hear: "You spend so much time with your head in a book." In another society that was good, but within our society it was not always considered good. The fact that it wasn't the right book — maybe it was another book, but nobody ever suggested that, they just felt that your head was in a book. They say, "Look at the white man," always saying, "Look at the white man." But the white man has something more to offer in that there is education in his background. Some of us, we're the first generation to get educated. You've got to come from so far and you've got to go so far. Educating takes thirty years, but who's prepared to support you for thirty years?

Some of them can't even send the children to public school, so any thought of a second or third level of education is not there. The streaming of Black kids will continue until the parents fight it more. It's only at the parent level that they're going to change it.

Esther H.: If the mother feels, "My son is not doing as well as he should, but I can't go to the school and speak to the teacher because it's their system," she hasn't that confidence in herself. Some who have an education, now they've gone to the other extreme. They don't need men — they don't need anything. But that's not it.

Even in the past Black people didn't have it. Take for instance Marcus Garvey. I was a follower of Marcus Garvey: we served at the table when he was up there, and we were at the meeting when he was up there. What I felt from meeting Marcus Garvey was that there

was hope for the Black man. The mayor of the
city was there at the meeting, and Garvey was
able to say something which amused
everybody — and the hall was packed with
people — and that turned the mayor's blood
red. But you don't build on that.

I don't know where they get those young
people today. Talking about streaming, I was
at one of those meetings at the board of education. You'd get a Black person coming up and
saying, "Our kids are not doing well because
of the prejudice and discrimination." That's
only part of it. You almost get the impression
that the school has more influence on the
children than you do. If you're not at home,
you're not teaching them anything. The thing
is self-confidence. I'm not saying that you're
not having any problems after that. But you
say, "Well, I could do it."

For instance, the time that Mr. Gairy's son
couldn't get in the roller skating rink on Yonge
Street we met up there and we had placards.
That was good. We got a bit of publicity. At
that time the Communist party would help us.
We could use their office. They would be using
us, but we didn't have enough members of the
community who could stand up to them. The
people that had the greatest influence in the
community all had the Communists behind
them. That would be 1940. Of course, they
didn't recognize Communists as being negative, as they do now. The Communists had the

supplies, they had the office, would run things off on their machine and all that.

You can't start from the top. It was attempted years ago, but it failed years ago. Let's move on, let's move on. But we're not moving on, we're not moving on.

Eleanor H.: My sister published a directory for thirteen years — a directory of Negro businesses in the city for thirteen years — and yet, someone was here just five minutes, and they think they started it.

Esther H.: I had over one thousand families on my mailing list — that's across Canada — and they would send for the Negro Directory. We used to see Black people on the street, and we used to get their name and number right down. If we knew about any organizations or clubs, we'd say, "Give us your calendar. If we could have your name or address or your calendar we will publish it. No charge." We sent out hundreds of directories.

Eleanor H.: But then when my sister stopped nobody picked it up. Esther started the directory in 1963.

Esther H.: We were all born in Toronto, born downtown — down around Queen and Beverley. We went to school on Spadina. At that time there were a large number of Jews at the school and a reasonable number of Negroes. They had a teacher at school who used to say, "There's only one Negro doctor. Why would you want to get an education? There's only one Negro doctor — he couldn't employ all of you." And a teacher would also say to another teacher, when they were marking books, "It looks like it's going to rain because it's cloudy," and that kind of thing.

Very few Negroes owned homes at that time. Those that got a place to live were usually in a home owned by Jews. In some ways, I feel that the Jews and the Negroes were close: they were depressed and we were depressed. Every now and then they would fight against us. Take, for instance, when you're going to school: if you had a fight with a Jewish boy, the parents would usually tell them, "You don't fight with Blacks." Their parents had a feeling for Blacks, but their children felt like the other children.

Eleanor H.: As neighbours we got along very well, but at the school, or at play, it was usually a different thing. In the neighbourhood our parents knew the parents across the street.

In school there were other people coming into the group, and they had their prejudices, and their prejudices affected the other ones.

Esther H.: Another thing, they had a saying that a Jew is a Negro with his white side out, and a Negro is a Jew with his black side out. In other words, they were having the same difficulty. Sometimes you would find a Jew that would really give you a chance, or try to give you a chance. Of course, you're still a little lower than an ordinary white person. I remember, too, my mother saying that she had taken us to her church once — I've forgotten which church it was; we were living here at St. George — and we were told that the minister at St. George's said that they felt that we would be happier at our own church.

The teachers in primary school could give you a hard time. I don't know if it's because we were poor. Of course, we were poorly dressed and that kind of business.

Eleanor H.: By today's standards the area would be called a disaster area. It was a very poor area — even the rich people were poor! It was just that type of place.

There wasn't a lot of Black people living around there at the time. There wasn't a lot anywhere.

Esther H.: But there were pockets of them. There were pockets here, and a pocket there, and the next pocket was way out east.

Eleanor H.: When we were young there was fifty Black families in the whole city. If you saw a Black anywhere, any place, you spoke.

Esther H.: One reason why you spoke was because your mother probably knows their mother. You see a Black woman on the street — and she may not call you, she may not speak to your mother on the phone — but if you pass her by and don't even speak, she's going to phone. Then you spoke to everyone, but when they started to flood in many years later you would come home, "I saw a Black person!" All you've got to do is raise your hand, you don't know who they are.

Another thing, most of the people that were working — the women at least — were doing housework. Even when you left school you did housework. Very few went on to high school because you weren't encouraged. I couldn't say there was discrimination in the high school, but you weren't encouraged to go to high school. If you did want to get anyplace, you went to the United States; if you went to the United States, you didn't come back. So it was always saved like that.

Yet a person would come from Africa and get into university here. True, there was a certain amount of discrimination against Africans, but they knew they were going back. So people get the impression that they come here, and they are accomplishing things that we Black Canadians didn't accomplish. We would've accomplished it.

Eleanor H.: But there again, they had a higher educational background — regardless of where they were coming from, they had that background that made it important to them to go on with their education. So the ones here who didn't go on, it's not just because they were here — they did not have that in their background; they did not have that in their history, in their family.

People coming from China or Vietnam and all, they have the background from home. They're not coming here as peasants and then rising to that level in one generation. You have to start farther back.

Esther H.: I believe that the women in the past had hope and they were so decent — too decent.

Eleanor H.: Those women would have socials up at the

hall at the UNIA. They would put on a social of some sort and charge you two cents. Of course, we had to scrounge around for this two cents for this social evening. These are the pennies they used to buy the hall with.

Esther H.: We also had Black Cross nurses with Garvey's group. We used to take first aid — the St. John's Ambulance course. First aid and home nursing. And we had white dresses, of course. Everybody had to make their own dress. When Marcus Garvey came the Black Cross nurses were all there.

Eleanor H.: The UNIA was sort of a centre when we were young, a centre run by adults. Then, anything that was put on was put on by adults, and the children were forced to go. So you got respect for them.

Esther H.: You had to have respect for them 'cause they were West Indian parents. Regardless of what they went through at home, they had respect for older people. But nobody has respect for anybody anymore. If you go to the hall, you don't shuffle around. You don't shuffle around because someone's going to stand up there and lay your soul to rest in front of everybody else. You just don't do it.

The UNIA was strong — the group in Montreal was also strong and a group across the border; they had connections, so when they had the convention, everybody and his dog was there — Marcus Garvey and all his men was there. All this gold braid, and they don't have a country in this world! He had a hat like Napoleon.

Eleanor H.: He sat in that chair, that big chair. He was about this big, he wasn't very tall. There was more chair than him! When he sat there, there was still more chair over him than under him, and when he sat up he was powerful, he was all powerful.

Esther H.: We sang, *"Ethiopia, the land of our fathers, the land where the gods love to be,"* and then we would always open the meeting with *Lift Every Voice and Sing*.

Eleanor H.: That was the Negro Youth Club singing. That is a beautiful piece. The words were very beautiful. The Negro Youth Club was the offshoot of Garvey's meetings. When we got older — I guess we were in our early teens — then we started doings things for ourselves. The women even used to put on dances for the young people. This Negro Youth Club was very large and very well run. We used to have annual debates and annual plays, socials — anything. At that level it was so well run because it was run by young people — it was the offshoot of Garvey, so they had that training. If only there had been someone around at that time to emphasize education, do something about it, it would have made a vast difference.

The only thing that helped some of the people get an education was the outcome of the war. When the war broke out and the boys went into the army and got their training — some of them did well with that. The war helped in some areas, but then in another area it sort of divided the community.

Esther H.: The youths would go up to the hall and report of the troubles Black people were having in getting into the army or getting into the air force. They didn't want you in the army. My own brother, my oldest brother, had to leave Ontario in order to get into the army, and then he was in four years. But they didn't want Black people in the army — it was a white man's war.

Blacks wanted to go into the army because there was no employment. If you didn't go into the army, you'd work on the railroad. Every mother hopes their son would not be a porter. Every mother hopes her daughter would be a nurse.

Eleanor H.: Those who wanted to be a nurse had to go to the States — you couldn't train here.

Esther H.: I see these women: you talk to them sometimes and they tell you they're struggling, and their children are pulling them one way, and they're pulling, and the women still go on.

We all worked domestic work, in service. There was a certain amount of pride to say, "This dress — the lady I worked for gave me this dress." Meaning it's an old dress, but the lady thought enough of you to give you her old dress.

Eleanor H.: We were talking about it once with a group — some of us who have been there and can talk about it without shame. One woman was saying how much she was getting paid, and she was getting five dollars a week in old clothes. If you were lucky — if the lady was nice — five dollars a week and old clothes.

Back then I worked for fifteen dollars a month, with carfare. That's nothing! They used to say with carfare or without carfare. A friend of mine was getting twenty dollars a month, but she didn't get carfare. Tokens were four for a quarter.

Esther H.: There was a Negro doctor in Toronto and he wanted a girl to work in his office. I applied for it — I was working someplace else, and I was getting eighteen dollars a week — and he couldn't pay me that much. He said, "Don't leave your job because I couldn't pay you that much."

Everything was much cheaper. The way the prices of houses are going now! We think it's terrible now. When we bought this place the place was much cheaper than they are now, but then the salary was so low. It's always a struggle — there never was a time when the cost of living and the income was equal — never.

Eleanor H.: When I was in high school the girls who wanted to take commercial courses or secretarial courses, they weren't encouraged to do so. We were told, "Well, who would want to hire you?" There were a few businesses that would hire you but very, very, very few!

There are women today living here in Toronto who were the first this and the first that: the first Black secretary in the government is living today; the first Black nurse to train in a hospital is living today; the first Black to work in Eaton's is living today.

Esther H.: We grew up with this kid who worked in Eaton's. She was working in the section doing West Indian imports — hats and things like that.

We used to go downtown just to see her. You wouldn't speak to her — you didn't want to upset the store, you know! — and she would never pass you by.

Eleanor H.: But we wouldn't do anything to jeopardize her job. George Carter, the judge, his wife was the first Black to be hired downtown.

When I left high school and was looking for a job I used to think I was good in figures. I took a dressmaking course because they already told me that nobody was going to hire me anyhow. And there again, there was nobody at home saying, "Go anyhow!" So I figured I'd settle with dressmaking, but when I got out of school I decided I didn't want to do that — I would like to try something else; I would like to work in a bank. So I got the phone book and I wrote down the number of all the branches downtown — Bay, Yonge, King, Adelaide, that whole bit — and I phoned each one: "Are there any jobs available?" "Oh yes."

Esther H.: "Are you prepared to hire a Negro?" "Oh no!" You would ask so as not to waste your time because there was carfare to consider.

Eleanor H.: Even if it was four tickets for a quarter, who

has the quarter? Then some girls coming up from the West Indies walked right by me and got in there. The scales go like this: at one point, a Black coming from the West Indies was taken before you.

The highest-paying job was porter, and porters obtained a bit of glory and independence when they formed a union. Unfortunately, that didn't carry over into anything else — it stayed within the porters' group.

Esther H.: The women were never too advantaged by being married to a porter. Then it got to the point where the people out east thought they were better than people downtown — and I guess they were because if they were porters they dressed well and they got steady income.

Eleanor H.: When we were slowly breaking out of that domestic environment there were an influx of Blacks from the east coast, and the West Indies who came in specifically to do the housework that we were trying to get away from. There was a bit of resentment that we thought we were getting somewhere and then to have them come in and do the same thing!

Esther H.: There was a group that started in Toronto — I believe it was all men to start with — and they were trying to increase the number of Black people able to come to Canada. I heard about it, so I went to one of their meetings. At the time the government was allowing less than a dozen Blacks into Canada! The community worked and worked and worked. We did something, but nothing holds on, nothing. If you have a glass of water — a glass of pink water — and you put more water in, you get more water, but you don't get any more pink. The thing is that you get these influxes every now and then, and then you lose what you done before.

Eleanor H.: And forgive me if I sound prejudiced, but when the West Indian girls started coming up and working as domestics — highly educated girls coming in — that really did it. Because number one, if you're a Canadian-born child of a West Indian family, you could never reach the heights of the West Indians left back home. To see that we were trying to get ahead and then have these girls — some of them wouldn't touch it with a ten-foot pole — do housework!

Esther H.: Another thing, those people who came in — they know they are above housework. They got the wrong attitude. They know they are better educated than you are because we went from housework into factory work.

Eleanor H.: That's where the openings were — garment factories or knitting mills — anything that wasn't too, too visible. The excuse they had was that the other employees might object. Now you hear them say that there's no discrimination here, but it's beneath the surface. But it wasn't beneath the surface then — they were very, very frank about it.

Esther H.: There were dance halls in Toronto and they would not allow Blacks in, period. They would bring a Black band from the United

States, and the band would come here and play, but you were not allowed in. So we picketed several of these places. Then it got to the point where the white man could sell you a ticket, but when they hand you the ticket they let you know you're not allowed in. They had to sell you the ticket, but when you came to the dance they would give you your money back.

Eleanor H.: One time I phoned the American embassy for a job. They had an ad in the paper, and I phone them and told them my qualifications. They said that would be nice, so I says, "Is it of interest to you as well that I'm a Negro?" "A Negro! Oh no, we couldn't hire you!" and they hung up. A little while later I got a phone call from the embassy saying that there had been some misunderstanding. "You're quite free to come down." I just told them where to put this job — I didn't go there. Americans in Canada, they felt free to say that.

Esther H.: It was a time when Paul Robeson would be coming to Toronto, and he would be having a meeting with the Black community at the Home Service Association — they had a community centre on Bathurst — and everybody came. And he used to sing. We could touch him.

Eleanor H.: And then again, the Home Service had a choir. Grace Price Trotman had this choir, the Negro Youth Choir, at the Home Service — beautiful! A very, very good choir of young people — and we used to sing with the Jewish Folk

Choir. Very, very good. One year the Jewish Folk Choir and the Negro Youth Choir sang in the Maple Leaf Gardens with Paul Robeson. I was in the choir and I sang. My voice joined with his!

Esther H.: We had a Negro orchestra. I think they performed one year only.

Eleanor H.: One person has an ambition, but you need more than one. There was one wanted an orchestra — and there was one who wanted this and one who wanted that — and there was never enough support.

Esther H.: For instance, Martin Luther King in the United States had a vision, but Martin Luther King could not carry it on past that. Someone had to carry on. What we don't have here is someone to carry on. We used to have Negro Youth Celebrations and a Negro Youth Week. We used to get together and plan. We had a Negro school at the church, once Negro history of music, Negro history of art — various things like that. When you had those meetings you had them at different churches and everybody went. You would have a young person who would get up there and read poetry by Paul Laurence Dunbar — there is no poetry like Paul Laurence Dunbar. You would have people who played piano, selections written by Negroes — they played any instrument. You knew your history through this because everybody went. You played the piano, and you were asked to take part in the programme, and then you had to learn a piece written by a Black.

Eleanor H.: The name of the orchestra was the Coldridge Taylor Symphony Orchestra.

Esther H.: My mother was very patient, but she never really understood the education system. And, of course, she had five of us and one foster brother, so the struggle was getting these children clothed and fed. She really didn't take part in community things, and she had a full-time job. We lived in a house, and we had these other parts of the house rented in order to pay the rent. I think she already had hopes for us, but she couldn't direct us.

Eleanor H.: There was this knowledge that education was very important, but no idea of how you went about it. She would say, "Your head is always in a book!" In some societies that's a good indication of something, but there was never that to suggest that you go on or to find somebody to help you. I think she was a typical Black mother at that time — subconsciously knowing that something was to be done but quite unable to do it. So many of the parents in our generation were the first generation to get an education. So many!

Esther H.: Both my mother and father taught us respect for older people and disregard for racism. They were never negative. They were always hoping — they didn't know how you were going to get there, but they were hoping you would get there.

Eleanor H.: Because Garvey was there it wasn't something

214 • No Burden to Carry

that had to be manufactured. He was the only person whose name would appear on anything without a crime being attached to it — when you saw a Black picture in the newspaper you didn't have to read anything, you know this man's in trouble. Garvey spoke out and he was highly visible. At the time the adults were listening to him, and they are the ones who subconsciously or otherwise train us.

Esther H.: I never felt that I wanted to be a follower of Garvey. He had his ideas and I didn't necessarily agree with them. The main thing I got from him was it was possible you could do something, not necessarily the way he did it because that wasn't the way I wanted to do it. My feelings towards him changed completely that day that he embarrassed that mayor. Nothing, nothing justified that, but he gave me the impression that with all my study of Negro history I can do something.

I was in the Negro Youth Club. We had a group in Toronto about the time of the Second World War, the Negro Youth Council. We had a little newspaper; we called it the *Council Drum*. The council was made up of representatives from various groups and then we would plan from there. It was a good idea, but this person and that person went to the United States, or to the west, where they could go ahead.

Eleanor H.: The first change in the community that I can remember — I remember feeling it physically

— was when the Second World War broke out and the boys were going into the army. Jobs were available for the girls because there were ammunition factories and what not, and these jobs were being filled. I can remember so well one evening being up in the hall — a social was going on — and there were very few people there. The hall felt empty.

That night there was a blackout. We were dancing and they had to put out the lights. Everything was just petered out and it was never the same after that. Before the war we stuck together because no one was working, or those who were working were working for twenty dollars a month, so we were together. But when other opportunities became available things just seemed to fall way. It was a very, very odd feeling.

Grace Price Trotman put on operettas, Gilbert and Sullivan (laughter)!

Esther H.:   They were beautiful and no amateur show was this. Everybody looked forward to this.

We had another group called the Women's Union. The Redmonds started the group and they were a little more advanced than we were.

Eleanor H.: Financially, a hell of a lot more advanced (laughter)!

Esther H.:   Some friends of Grace Price Trotman were in that and Bee Allen was. Mrs. Stanfield was also with it; she was a dietitian and worked in a hospital. The Women's Union had this group of young people.

Eleanor H.: They wanted to make ladies of us, but not in

a condescending way. At that particular time, it was a very, very good influence on me.

Esther H.: They would take you to their house for tea or something like that. They had houses and everybody else was living in a flat.

Eleanor H.: One woman in particular would take the time to try to make something of us — we were rowdy, but that she would even take the time to come down to the place was something. At first we played tricks on her and all that sort of thing. She was very proper, and that just encourages you to do more to her. But she was deeply interested, and she wasn't being condescending or anything like that. I was making a dress for something that was coming up and she said she'd help me. So I got my dress together, and I went all the way up to her house — almost needed a passport to get there! And she took the time to show me how to finish the dress. She was a person I never would have met under other circumstances. I think of her so often. It makes you realize that even if you don't have much you can help somebody.

The women who used to run the UNIA Hall, I think of them as looking up to them. There was Mrs. Braithwaite, and Edna Braithwaite's mother, Mrs. Bristol, and her mother, Mrs. Meyers. There was Mrs. Ethel Holdip — we gave her a fit! There was Mrs. Benjamin. They had a choir that used to sing at the hall, and Mrs. Meyers played the piano, and if she hit the keys, that was all right!

Esther H.:   They used to have these meetings at the hall
when young people were called to think about
Negro history. I've only written one poem and
it was about Marcus Garvey. It was published
in the newspaper, *The Black Mag*. The thing is,
I wrote it, and I stood up, there and I read.
There's no places like that today. Mr. Pitt was
president of the UNIA. He was a lawyer, and
he would stand up there, and he would tell
you, "Next week I want you to speak of something," and you did it. If you could play *Chop-
sticks*, and somebody knew you could play it,
you played it. Out of respect for adults you
weren't going to mess up. You weren't going
to not turn up. That was important — the fact
that the adults were so involved in it.

They had a girls' basketball team, and the
girls were really enjoying themselves playing
with the basketball. I remember one time I was
asked if I would supervise the girls at this
game — it might have been at St. Christopher
House. These girls were playing a team from
outside Toronto. They had a boy in charge,
and he said to me, "Gee, your kids are good.
Why don't they practice?" His team were
young people going to school and they had a
gym to practice in. I say, "They're young girls,
but they're working girls. Their future probably is not as good as your team's. They have no
place to practice, but yet they are playing."
Our kids were the same age, but they had to
be responsible for they're working. They're
not going to school.

This Black Power thing that came to Toronto, it really, really stabbed the Black community. It was so negative. They moved into the Home Service and the destroyed the place physically. And the African thing. They were learning Swahili. I thought it was so negative.

What has come out of it? It didn't do anything positive. The idea could have been used in the groups that were here, in directing them rather than going and blasting them. You get to know your history, which is good, but in order to do that you put down somebody else's. You don't do it that way; it's a negative thing. I'm wondering how many members of the Black *Canadian* community took part in it. I believe it was more the newcomers, whether they were from the United States or West Indians. Not many Canadians that I knew of took part in it.

Eleanor H.: I don't see it as totally negative because I feel some people needed it. Some of them needed some form of identification, and it served the purpose for that. It wasn't for everyone — nothing is — but it was more positive for some than others.

Esther H.: I believe it had no regard for what we've done. It was separate to what was done.

Today I believe the women are too pushy; they've gone to the other extreme; they're being man and woman. And the men are irresponsible — that's the way they were raised. The women are demanding. When anybody tells me "demand" I stop listening. I can see you can ask for a thing; you can press for a thing, or work towards a thing, but demanding is out. I just find it very jarring, very jarring. They're over-killing when they have nothing to base it on, or when they do not have people to carry it out. They are threatening and they have nothing. If they were a little more sensible about it, they might get help rather than give the impression that we have the power. Women don't have the power. We need help to do this.

Eleanor H.: When I hear women say that they were raised to cater to men, and they're being kept in the kitchen and all that sort of thing, I always think it doesn't apply to Black women. I don't feel Black women are raised that way at all. When I was younger I felt that the women were equal. I think women are stronger now than when we were younger, but I don't know that it's good because, as my sister has indicated, it has made the men weaker. I think too much responsibility has been taken from them. It's all right to have one foot in the kitchen and the other in the office, but it's at the expense of the men.

I would rather see more equality of strength than the women being everything for everybody. I don't like it because I think the family suffers. The family unit suffers because the women are into everything, and the man — if he's there at all — can walk away, and the structure doesn't collapse because he wasn't part of the structure.

Rella Braithwaite
1923

My mother was born in Elmira, Ontario, in 1888; my father in 1886.

Their parents came to Canada and settled in that area called the Queen's Bush; that's where they settled.[1] I can't say exactly, but about the time I was born we had moved a little further west.

I remember my father was telling us about how he courted my mother in a horse and buggy. My father was born in Kingston, and his father came to Canada from the West Indies — Barbados — in the 1870s; now as far as we know, they were free people when they came, and he married an American woman. They then settled there in the Queen's Bush area.

My mother's folks came up from the States; they came from the southern states to the Pennsylvania Dutch area, then on up through the northern states and then through to Canada.[2] They came as free people, as far as we can remember back. Quite a few, quite a few Blacks were held there and came up by way of the Underground Railroad — they said that they received so much help from the Pennsylvania Dutch people.

I distinctly remember on my mother's side they had a very large farm — 200 and 300 acre farms — 'cause she's always told us. They farmed grains; I remember they'd have great big thrashings, and they were living amongst the German people. The people in that area, a great many of them were Mennonites, and even my father could speak some German. My mother said how the people were friendly, very friendly: she would say when they had these great big thrashings they always said that Mrs. Lawson — my mother's name was Mary Lawson before marriage — was such a good cook and baked so many nice pies. They would all take turns helping each other when they had these thrashing or these big jobs on the farms: the men would help each other; the women would help each other.

My mother grew up in a family of seventeen children, but she used to say, "Well, we had all the products on the farm to support ourselves." And they all helped: you didn't get very much assistance in those days.

Then, as her brothers got older, they bought farms on their own. They were bachelors; I can remember them being bachelors for many years and running their own farms. But she always mentioned the big farms that they had and the amount of food that they produced themselves, like the milk, butter, eggs — they had plenty.

My father was an only child and he worked very hard as a labourer. He didn't really have skills when he got married and so he worked very, very hard. We had seven acres. Seven acres. We lived on that for twenty-some years, in Elmira. We moved further to Listowel, and that's where I grew up: Listowel, Ontario.

We had a great big field garden and you had to weed; I can remember, definitely, long rows up in the gardens, and then there beans that you shell, and you put them away for the winter. You'd do all of those jobs.

Houses weren't insulated, not like they are today. You're cold, but you build a fire, and you sit around the fire in the morning until the house gets warm; you'd have this big stove and good heat comes out of them, but it takes a while to warm up. I was fortunate because I had both parents together all the time and we did own our own home. We always owned our own home, but I think that Blacks had a harder time that were living in cities. And then, if they didn't have two parents.... I was lucky because we stayed right at this one place, which was just a little frame house and seven acres. That's quite a fair amount of land.

Sometimes, in the small places like that, you sell most of what you farm, like we made our own butter and we had a separator. I helped, but the rest were older, and I can remember the oldest boys doing the separator; I was pretty small for my age so I got away without doing too much!

There had been a sizeable Black community there, but gradually they dispersed. Some of our cousins lived in the next town, so we were fortunate in that respect: we weren't all together, but we could visit. Listowel wasn't that far from Stratford; some cousins would come from Stratford and London, Ontario and other areas that our relatives lived because there was so many relatives, coming from that large family. I do remember that whole area was mainly Irish and Scotch-English.

I marvel at how my mother managed on our seven-and-a-half acres. Now we had a couple of cows and some chickens ourselves. My father didn't get home from his job on time, so she would milk those cows and do the chores, look after the chickens and that. And yet she was always involved in women's groups; she would be president of this and president of that. The Ladies Aid was quite an important one. And we went to the United Church, which was a white church, but she was always involved. After my older sisters came to the city of Toronto and got involved with the BME Church, then I can remember my mother coming down frequently to conferences and things, and we would get all the news about the Black church in Toronto.

There were seven in our family and I was the third youngest. We had four boys and three girls. It seemed very natural to her; she enjoyed all the activities, even with a family having that many children. I guess the older ones looked after the younger ones, but she was always involved.

My mother always wanted to be a schoolteacher, and I can remember her helping the various members of the family with their studying and their homework. She was quite progressive in that way. My father was self-taught, just from reading. My mother did have a fair amount of education for that time. But she was quite a progressive woman, and she was never a bored woman, even living in the country. Never bored. She was busy; she seemed to enjoy her life. But sometimes I think if I had to live in the country today, I'd probably find it depressing; but no, she was happy. She just made herself happy and I think that's what we have to do.

In the farming community where I grew up, of course, the women did not go out to work. But the area where my Black relatives lived, in the various towns, the women would be taking in laundry and going out and doing work of maids, which was prevalent in Toronto.

Now I went to high school after growing up and going through the one-room schoolhouse. My sister Dorothy —

just two years younger than myself — and I, we were always the first in our class.

But at twelve years of age I found myself in the quite large high school, all white. I was quite shy 'cause I was very small for my age. I went there for a couple of years. It was quite a thing in the wintertime: I had to board in a house in town and I remember one of my older brothers helped to pay the board; I was quite anxious to go to a big city where my older sisters had gone.

Being the only Black child in the school — O Mary! — I didn't function that well. Somehow I was not impressed with strangers; I just didn't feel that comfortable.

I was born in 1923. It must be late, definitely the late '30s, when I came to Toronto. By that time you would take a train, but the connections wouldn't be too good, and the money to get to travel the train — it was hard to get.

My older sisters were down in Toronto first, and I came down at the age of fifteen. Immediately, my older sister taught me how you could be a mother's helper. In the city of Toronto I was with my eldest sister — the one who's a minister, Addie — and she taught me. I was not accustomed to it — and then as soon as I got into little jobs, I attended many night classes. Very soon after that I started taking night courses and went to business college to take and learn as much as I could.

I enjoyed my childhood. As we got older, we wanted to be where there were more Blacks, but I enjoyed my childhood very much. My mother and father were both there: they lived together for over fifty years. We had close friends with the white children, but I seemed anxious to come to the big city; I was raring to come to the big city!

The first job that you could get, you took. At that time they were advertising for cook generals — and that was the older women; the older women knew how to do all the cooking and look after a household — and that's what my two older sisters were. But when you were young as my age you were a mother's helper.

Thursday was quite the day. It was a very busy day at the hairdressers'— that was women's afternoon off. There were some big dances, too, on Thursday. Special dances, seemed to me, that some of them were, and at that time they also had midnight show.

After I got in the city and attended night classes, and I had experience, I wanted to get out of housework — being a mother's helper, you did some housework with that besides looking after children. I wanted to get away from that. I tried factory and I detested that. I was at the factory at Wellington Street in Toronto: they wove some kind of twine; you operated these machines, and you walked around all day and kept these machines going, and it was very noisy. Then I worked at a place making Christmas decorations on Queen Street. This would be in the early '40s and I didn't enjoy those jobs at all, either.

It wasn't easy to get into the factory. Not easy. I think that they were just starting then getting Black women. Mainly domestic work was available. But I definitely wanted to get away from factory work after I got into that.

I think I must've been around nineteen before I got a job that I really liked. There was a place called National Selective Service, down on Queen and Spadina, and it was where the people registered for changing jobs; they'd go there to get good jobs, and I was a filing clerk there. I wasn't really typing that well, but just because I had taken typing and shorthand I was able to get a job there. Before that, of course, other places they were taking real light ones. It was a very large building. There were three Blacks there — Inez Perry, Ursula Clarke and I. A sister of mine worked in a war plant. Then after that the war was on, and I met a soldier and married at the age of twenty.

Quite a few Black people went into the service from Metro, and then many came here to Toronto from all over. It was quite the thing for these soldiers. You'd meet new soldiers on the street all the time; they tried to have some shelters and places for them at some of the churches, and some people took them into their homes.

My husband was born in Montreal of Barbadian parents and grew up in Montreal, but he was stationed at Camp Borden, so he would come to Toronto for the weekends, and that's how I met him. I think my sister met him first. She'd met a group of soldiers. She took him to one older sister's home, and then I met him. We seemed to get along. We married in 1943, quite a long time ago.

I was two months under twenty when I got married. It was different then, because they didn't concentrate on careers, and if you weren't married it would be strange. Used to be that you were an old maid or a spinster.

Nineteen forty-three was the time when most of the Blacks lived around the Spadina and Dundas and Queen area, and you scarcely went above Bloor to shop or anything: you wouldn't feel at ease and you wouldn't be treated too well; at that period of time you just felt quite out of place. At that time there were no Black businesses; the first businesses would be the barber shops and women's hairdressing. Black women's hairdressing parlours have been here for many years.

The church played a very important role, much more important than today. That's where you went to meet people. They'd even stand outside the church and socialize. In my early days I remember Mme. Brewton would teach youth on the Bible, and then she would have social functions at her home, up in North Toronto. Her husband, Dr. Brewton, was a foot specialist and she was a beautician. She had a beautiful beauty shop on Yonge Street, and she got quite a few of us young ones involved in her Bible classes after church on Chestnut Street in Toronto.

When I first came to Toronto it was kind of nice to see all the Blacks so close together in the central area of Toronto. The Black people, we knew each other; everybody knew everybody. They were close, with the exception of a few families that were better situated and did live up a bit north. Some of the families were probably mixed, but otherwise everybody knew each other, and they really were close. Also the UAIA, which was then the UNIA, played a very important role. I went to the activities — the Saturday night dances with the records were very enjoyable. I do remember hearing a lot about Marcus Garvey at the UNIA. I wasn't at the meeting, but I can remember him coming. I remember reading about it in the *Africa Speaks* paper. I wrote for *Africa Speaks* for a while. It was a little paper.

The UNIA building was right on College Street. I had many good times there. I remember Mme. Brewton used to tell my girlfriend that we couldn't go there because you may not meet very nice people, but we enjoyed that. And the Home Service Association played an important role also.[3]

Soldiers would go there, and they'd have socials and food. The main churches were the BME, the AME on Soho Street, which is still on Soho Street, and the Baptist, which at the beginning was on Edward Street; but during the war, there was a Reverend Stewart started a church on Elm Street, and that was a church that the soldiers would go to.

I was married. The second year of the war I was expecting a child. At that period you did not keep your job when you were expecting, but I didn't feel well from the beginning. You would feel out of place if you weren't feeling well and you were expecting, so I immediately gave my notice.

My husband was overseas a couple of years. All of the men remember that they went overseas and gave up jobs, or lost out on education and everything, and when they came back it was very hard to get a job. He retrained when he came back, along with the rest of the soldiers, but it was not easy. He remembers the long line up when they came back: nearly everybody else white and he was standing in it — he and one other Black soldier. They pointed right to my husband, and they called him up to the front, and they told him right away: "You! You go to the porters and get a job there." They just picked him right out of the line up like that, but he really didn't want to go there.

Afterwards, he did train with Ryerson, but when he went to train they would tell him: "But you won't get a job at sheet metal work." It was true: at that time most Black men could only get jobs on the railroad. My husband worked as a porter for a very short time, just so many months.

Eventually we moved out here because we had one child and another on the way, and we wanted to have more space. We lived in the east end of Toronto in a flat, which was quite common at that time.

You just seemed to know where to go or not to go — the only place that you could get, it was central. The Jewish were down in that area, Beverley-McCaul. Jewish people would rent to Black people — we must remember that, we sometimes forget. A lot of them were the early type of Jews, the Jews that came from Europe, and then a lot of them were the professional people. They were the only ones that would rent to Blacks. I suppose that they remembered when they were discriminated against. Another reason was they happened to operate those businesses right down in that area: the restaurants, the doctors, everything.

My husband did get assistance from the Veterans' Land Act in buying a half-acre. He was told to look for a place and we soon found this place — a half-acre and a little house. We're still here.

When we got to Scarborough there was a new plant going up, which was the John Mansfield plant, and he was there for three years, around 1947. He's very lucky to be alive today. He was carrying bags of asbestos, and it was the asbestos plant which just had so much bad publicity.[4] The main number of men that worked have already passed on, so he's fortunate that he didn't stay longer than three years.

There weren't that many Blacks that came out of the city to live, so not many Black men worked there; but all the white men have gone on, and it's had an awful lot of bad publicity. At that time it was a big beautiful plant and you were so pleased to get on.

After three years, then, he was discouraged because there was no way that he could work his way up. He would see all these white friends — some of them weren't even skilled — and they would go up the ladder. After three years he left, and he started on his own in the scrap metal business, and he's still in it today, thirty-some years afterwards.

We had six children. Everybody was building their own homes or else just living in some little simple place. In those days, the women would walk out a great deal with the children and get involved in community work: the Home and School Association — they honoured me as a life time member — and Salvation Army work, all kinds of volunteer work the women here would do.

It was isolated in Scarborough — it was isolated, definitely against Blacks — but there were white friendly people. A lot of them had come here after the war too, so we all pretty well felt the same until the children would get to be teenagers, and then they would hope that Blacks wouldn't mix with them, but the people were very nice. The girls were better at finding Black activities than the boys; the boys would have more opportunities of going out with a white girl — that's always the way. The boys would be more comfortable at the parties, but the girls wouldn't be quite welcome.

When my one son was sixteen, and I was helping him with a project, I said something about using Black heroes — especially women heroes, I meant — and he said, "Were there Black heroes? I didn't know there were any women heroes." About that time I had started going to the annual September labour day function at North Buxton because my eldest sister was ministering there. "Oh yes," I said, "I heard a lot about them when I went to North Buxton."

I had also started reading the book *Look to the North Star*, so I was collecting Black history by that time, and I got my son interested in it; then we all got more inquisitive to find more material, and it was about that time I started working in Black history. I really couldn't find too much. Then I got the idea of writing, and I phoned *Contrast* to know if I could write those Black history columns. In 1969, I think, their paper started, and the next year I was writing a column which I kept writing for several years.

I was quite enthused when I read about Harriet Tubman. We were quite interested in all Black history, but I more or less concentrated on women because I found there was so little done. I could find quite a bit of material from the States, but there was very little done in Canada at that time, so I got quite interested in if I could contribute in some way.

The late Kay Livingstone asked me to work on a little booklet for the first Congress of Black Women, with Enid D'Oyley, and that really got me right into writing something. I still can't understand how I got into it, but I really felt strongly that you needed more material.

Many of the Black people that were here helped to pave the way for the new immigrants that come in the country. And in another respect I think we were quite conditioned: we knew the area that we could stay in, and I think it really did something to us; I think our parents were just resigned to the fact that you were discriminated against. It really does something to you because you have to survive. And so I'm very thankful for the amount of immigrants and the professional ones that have come in and inspired us.

It was good that when all the Canadian Blacks got better jobs they moved out in various areas. It was good in one way. Some of them went on, and they just forgot about their race at the same time, so that's one of the negative factors. But they definitely advanced and progressed, which was necessary — it was necessary to do that.

In the early days — the '30s, the '40s — all the women, white and black, they were deprived all right. It was years of deprivation for women. It was hard to progress, and it was difficult even for the white women to get their formal education. The boys were supposed to get the most education, because they always said the girls they didn't need it. Things have changed very much for the better for women; there's no doubt about that. As far as women abuse, I just can't seem to recall too much of that, but I'm sure it probably was kept more hidden than today. I can remember some in the Black community, but it was probably more hidden, and we weren't aware if it was going on. Today we hear of them more, but I'm sure it's easier. It's much better for all women. There's no doubt about that.

I used to read books about the women's suffrage movement and that, but it didn't seem real. I was so young, I just couldn't believe that it was that bad. Black women — we just were so busy economically, trying to make a living. They had to work, and then they had the families. Also, our men would be lowly paid — and many of our men unemployed — so women would involve themselves trying to help the home financially.

Black women always want to find our identities or know ourselves better. When you speak of Black men — Black boys — we have to be very, very particular about raising our Black boys because we have too many unskilled, too many drop-outs, amongst our boys. I think there is a problem. We know right now that we are discriminated against, and it's hard enough to get work, but if they're unskilled and uneducated what hopes are there? I think once we're aware of it, we can concentrate on it more with our younger boys. It definitely does help for our Black boys to know their identity and they'll be better people for it. They just grow up so much in the white society.

When the Civil Rights movement started in the States it had quite a reaction here. Most of them beforehand were just glad to get by: you had such a hard time and our parents had a hard time, just glad to make a living. But we didn't have the pride in our race that we should've, and the Civil Rights movement really affected Canadian Blacks:

before our children would go to bed the children were all marching up and down the floor: "I'm Black and I'm proud, I'm Black and I'm proud." It was so funny when I think back. I remember that there was a whole awakening here — it really hit here in Canada, very strongly, about the pride of being Black. I think that was a necessary factor.

Notes

1. For a map of early Black settlements in Canada, see C. Peter Ripley, ed., *The Abolitionist Papers*, vol. II (Chapel Hill and London, The University of North Carolina Press, 1986), p. 16. *Papers* notes that:

    > By 1850 blacks had settled in six areas of Canada West: along the Detroit frontier, particularly at Windsor, Sandwich, Amherstburg, Colchester, and the surrounding region; in Chatham and its environs, including the all-black settlements at Dawn and Elgin; in the central section of the province, including London, Brantford, Queen's Bush, and the all-black Wilberforce settlement; on the Niagara frontier, particularly St. Catharines; in the urban centers of Hamilton and Toronto; and at the northern perimeter of Lake Simcoe.

2. "Pennsylvania Dutch" are descended from 18th-century settlers from southwest Germany and Switzerland. Pennsylvania had banned slavery by 1784.

3. The Home Service Association, organized to serve Black servicemen during World War I, expanded its work to include counselling, recreation and education for Blacks at home as well as for returning soldiers. See Winks, *op. cit.*, p. 319 and p. 421.

4. Asbestos is known to cause a form of cancer.

Marjorie Lewsey
1923

I was born in Toronto, 1923, at home. I'm a widow, mother of two daughters. My first school I went to would be what is now known as George Brown Campus on Nassau Street. It was called William Houston.

We didn't live there too long — we moved and my next school was Ryerson Public School. During those days, "nigger" was quite the word to be used, and there weren't that many of us. Consequently, we almost always ended up in the principal's office every day because my mother always told us it was the most derogatory term that could be used towards a Black person. There were some that just couldn't take the message — and there were about ten families who had children going to Ryerson Public School — and we all got it one way or another. My brother was forever fighting.

We were always addressed as "niggers." It was hard, I'm not kidding. The teacher used to put us under the window. Miss Burkholder. The reason she did that was because she said we smelled. I got double pneumonia. All the teachers in those days, except some men who taught in the higher grades, were women. Romeo Gaskins, Tex, Dorothy — we were always in the office.

We had Jewish groups in that area — they were around Nassau, Leonard, Bellevue — and they had a way of trying to make us feel very uncomfortable. Our only solace was St. Christopher House; we used to go there and more or less get together with the different ones that were allowed to go — play basketball, learn arts and crafts. It was sort of a way out — unwinding, especially after school. We rented. Why, we were moving all the time — Nassau, Lippincott, Bellevue.

Then again, we all met at 355 College Street, Sunday afternoons. It was from two o'clock, supposedly, until four; sometimes it went into six or seven at night, but that was when our parents and all of the children were up at the Universal Negro Improvement Association.

B.J. Pitt was the president, and every one of us had to get up and perform; if it was only reading a poem, we had to get up and recite.[1] We had to listen to Garvey's message to us as Blacks in a foreign land. We were encouraged to stand up for our rights. We had different speakers; some of the people that came there were from the Garvey movement in the States, where he was at the time. I remember as a child Garvey came, around 1929, '30 — my dad was still alive then. We children were up about seven o'clock in the morning to see and to listen to Marcus Garvey. I remember seeing the guard of honour: Marcus Garvey stepped out of a car, and the guards held their swords high as he walked under to go into the UNIA. I can't recall too much of what he said — I know we had to be very quiet. I heard a lot of clapping; I saw a lot of women crying. He did say that Africa was our home. Where Africa was I didn't know. I was about five or six years old. But it left an impression on me seeing this — he was a short man — being honoured the way he was: men standing at attention when he walked by; men listening to him; men standing and clapping when he spoke. I do remember asking my mom after about the Black Star Line, of which she bought shares. Both my mom and dad bought shares in the Black Star Line. It was a sad day, I remember, when they heard that Marcus Garvey was in prison. I couldn't make any sense of it — something about mail fraud, which didn't mean too much to me at the time, but it was very sad. My mother lost quite a bit of money — could've amounted to ten or twenty dollars, I don't know.

I also remember the Depression, and there was a lot of suffering. But we had one thing and that was a lot of love — because we were all poor. Not all — but the majority of us — were on welfare. I can tell you none of us ever went to bed hungry — because if it was one potato my mother had, and somebody had a piece of meat, she would share that potato with the person. I could call her name; she lived on our street, on Lippincott. But we had a lot of care. We all had a telephone — because at that time it was a dollar or two dollars a month — that was our communication. Plus going to the hall on Sundays. We still went — we had to go; that was all there was to it. If you were missing you got a phone call: where were you? I missed you at the meeting last Sunday. So there was a lot of caring and a lot of sharing that I witnessed as a child. Consequently, I'm a bit confused. Sometimes I'll sit and look back and think maybe it was better when we all didn't have two cars or have a two-car garage, or didn't have a home to call our own, 'cause we cared about our fellow man.

My mom came to Canada, I believe, in 1919 from Basseterre, St. Kitts. She was a grammar school teacher in St.

Kitts. You realize that Black women then, and, I guess, as now, had to come as domestics. I remember her telling me that she worked up there in the St. Clair area. Most of the women that came from the Caribbean had to find a church, had to find a Black church. My mother was very churchy, and quite a few of them working in and around that area went to Timothy Eaton Memorial Church on a Sunday morning for services. I have proof — even though she's not here — because there are other mothers that told their children that they went to church one Sunday, and whoever the minister was those days asked the Blacks not to come back, to take their nickels and dimes and go to their own church. Thereby hangs Timothy Eaton Church. So there was a lot of trying to figure out just what this land was all about.

Years later, I went there to see this place that my mother was asked to leave. A friend and I went in, but neither one of us could stay. I said, "I've had it." She said, "I'm out of here too." Canada is known as being subtle; you gotta be pretty stupid not to read between the lines.

Eventually, they did find their own church, which she was married in — St. James British Methodist Episcopal Church. I don't remember the street it was on. Then they moved to Chestnut Street, and that's where I was christened, 94 Chestnut Street, which I believe now is a Chinese church of some sort.

My mom told us how hard it was when she first saw snow; she cried because nobody told her it was going to be so cold here. All she knew was she was coming here to make a better life for herself and her family, and it was very, very hard. They worked from sun up.

My dad was from Barbados. He came, and the first thing that happened when he landed in Sydney was they put him in the army. It would be about 1914 when Daddy came to Canada, and they shipped him over to France — he didn't know what he was fighting for, or who he was fighting for, or just what was going on. That's where he was until 1918 when the war ended. I have his picture; I have his discharge paper.

Most of the people from the islands landed in Sydney.[2] Then, I guess, he heard there was more work up here in Toronto, and he sent for my mom. He was quite a race man, a Garveyite. He taught my brother and I about Garveyism, and my mother was one too. They were quite willing to stick with Garvey in his trek to take us all back to Africa.

Daddy says that a lot of the orders that they gave to primarily the Blacks, it was something else again: digging trenches, burying the dead, cleaning up whatever mess there was — it was just horrible. Although great things were promised to my dad when the war was over — they were all going to get a job; there was lots to be had — the only job my dad could find after searching for work for years was to become a porter on the CN car.

There were four of us children. I had two sisters; they were born in St. Kitts. My brother and I, we were born here. My mother worked to bring them here; at least, she felt it would be better here for them. She worked taking in children; she looked after other people's children, and that was about all she could do because she had Bobby and I to look after.

She wanted me to get an education, a good education, so I wouldn't have the life that she had. Her desire was to learn, to keep learning. Don't ever refuse to learn: learn how to play the piano; learn how to read and to write properly — that was her desire for both my brother and I.

She had a hard life, extremely hard, so much so that

December 25, 1934, my dad was called out to go to work because whoever had the main line wanted Christmas home, and my dad went in the regular man's place. He never came home anymore; he was killed instantly at Dundas, Ontario. As long as I live, I'll never forget the day. Somewhere up north they'd been going. The engineer switched the tracks. As they used to say in those days, the train had a hot box — they'd put it on the side. The train was powered by coal. Daddy's train was cooling off — the name of the train was the Maple Leaf Flyer.

The brakeman was a little high, and he switched tracks, not knowing that they'd already been switched for it to go past. By switching the track it put it on the same track where this train was standing still. It crashed right through Daddy's train. He was thirty-seven when he died.

When the man came to tell her to prepare for the worst — there'd been a train accident — my mother grew old overnight. Her prayer was to see my brother and I both grow and be able to take care of ourselves because workman's compensation at the time gave her forty dollars for herself, seven dollars a *month* for my brother and I until we reached the age of sixteen, and then we were automatically cut off. She used to get a grand total of fifty-four dollars per month. When we reached sixteen it was put right down to forty dollars. There was no place to fight — that was the way it was. Forty dollars until she passed away in '47. We weren't allowed to ask our parents their age — I found out going through her papers that she was fifty-nine when she died. Ask my mother how old she was — backhand.

At that time in school it was senior fourth, junior fourth. So I went to it would be grade eight at the time, going by the way we use the figures now. Then my mother lost her eyesight and I left school. I went out to work. I had to leave school at sixteen. There weren't too many jobs. The first job I had was working in a factory; the place was called Reliable Toy. Quite a few of the Blacks left the education system because there was no future for us. We knew it. I went out and worked at Reliable Toy. I think it was five dollars a week — that was big money in those days. I got married around twenty-two, twenty-three — somewhere in there.

After Reliable Toy, I worked in a factory down on John Street; they made suits. There was lots of that domestic work, going and cleaning up other people's dirty place. Really and truly, we weren't allowed to go into factory work until Hitler started the war, and then they'd beg you, "Would you like a job in my factory?" But we weren't allowed in. We were left more or less to clean their dirty houses. Which I *never* did, I'll tell you that. Then we had a chance to go and work in the ammunition dump. They called it GICO. That's where Centennial College is now — used to be the war plant. I lasted about a *week* there. I couldn't stay because I started to haemorrhage. It was filling magazines, little pellets with gunpowder for the soldiers. I kept menstruating — the humidity was too high or something, I couldn't stay. I have pictures of some of us that were out there. Grace Trotman was out there, Maisey, Shirley Plummer. There were many Black women out there. I had to go back to other factory work.

I worked Scholl's Footwear till about '75, '76. There was nothing here for us. Sometimes I have to smile at some of these people that just came, and they think, "Boy, we've opened doors." They're making it up as they go by the graveyard. Some of them are just tokens. Takes me two minutes to tell them. They were so desperate in the war they didn't bother you — there was no such thing as your race.

I was too young to hold office with the UNIA. I was just

more or less an adherent of the doctrines and policies of them. There were other Black women who held office in the organization. I just felt that the men weren't able to do the job the way that, say, Mrs. Blackman was able to do the job. There was Mrs. Braithwaite, who was Danny and Edna Braithwaite's mom — she was heavily involved — and Mrs. De Costa — she was very active in the movement. All these women — Mrs. Meyers, who would be Allen Meyers' mom — they were all very active. I remember them in the Black Cross nurses. Once a week I had to go up and help them make bandages to send to Africa. There was a war going on there; I don't know whether it was Ethiopia or where, but we made these bandages to send to them. I know we did it on the second floor because the third floor was more or less held for the Saturday night dances and the meetings.

There was the Oddfellows, but they held their meetings upstairs and left their regalia and so on downstairs, so I used to see them going upstairs. My dad was gone by then, but they all knew me; they knew my father, and it was, of course: "Go straight home."

I started getting involved in community activities because I saw there was a need coming in so far as saying to the young people there's a lot to be learned, a lot to be gained. When I took my course at Centennial College I had to do placements, and I preferred to do them in the Black community. I decided to go back to school because I felt working in the factories just wasn't what I had in mind or my mom probably had in mind, and she did try to instill in us to get an education. I thought: now that my family is grown, able to take care of themselves, what better chance? So I went back; I did the two-year course at Centennial, in social work. I also did a course in philosophy. I graduated from there, and I went to Children's Aid Society, but I didn't like that too much.

I found that I had no answers: I could not look at people and tell them that everything was going to be all right and know that just maybe it wouldn't be. I thought: well no, this is not for me; I'll have to get to where I can reach some of the parents of the children who may need help. I'm quite happy to say I found that place. Quite a few of the Black children I work with have gone on and have been able to see that there's another way.

I worked around organizations in the Black community, getting more or less what I call experience learning exactly just what was happening in the community. I worked with BRIC — the Black Resources and Information Centre[3] — for a while, and I was with Dave Clarke and the half-way house. I worked in there with him, trying to get things on an even keel, and basically just wherever I felt. I used to go and visit the Harriet Tubman Centre just to hear or to see how they were making out.[4] That would be about it until the last few years when I became more heavily involved in the political and community life.

I don't feel that running for a political office that I could do as much as I feel that I could do being a member of East York Federation of Ratepayers. I feel once I put on a mantle of belonging with the borough that I'm no longer any use, so consequently I've never had the desire to run for any municipal, federal or provincial seat. I am a member of the Federation of East York, delegate-at-large. I am past vice-president of the East York Multi-Cultural Race Relations Committee, and I enjoyed that because if people come — which they do — with any complaints, I'm able to find out the whys, and sometimes, what for.

The political and community organizations that I've

dealt with I will call them to whatever point I feel I'm being slighted, so consequently I've never witnessed sexism or felt that. I have witnessed it, but not me personally. I didn't give my daughters lots of advice that I couldn't afford about being Black women, but I did give them pride in themselves to know that they must not stand down for anybody. They feel that they're right for whatever that they may be doing. As long as they are not hurting anyone, stand up for that right. And if they do fall, get up and dust yourself off. Keep going: do not stand in one place and be browbeaten and taken advantage of; you have a lot to live and to learn. Keep going. It doesn't matter what anybody may think of you, they're not giving you anything — their thoughts are for free. Just stand up. I would like to see Black women become more cohesive. I would like them to share with one another, do something to help each other. We're so fractured now that we're unable to even contain ourselves, and a lot of us have anger and pain. But you don't know who to turn to because we are so fractured.

We're getting ready to present Garvey's chair to the JCA.[5] I promised Sister Blackman that the chair would be put in a safe place.

To the young Black woman I would say: hold your head high. To the young Black woman I would say: let nobody turn you around; there is a light at the end of the tunnel, but it's not coming to you; you have to go to it.

Notes

1. For more information on B.J. Pitt, see Winks, *op. cit.*, p. 417.

2. Sydney, Nova Scotia. In Nova Scotia, a segregated Black battalion was raised to serve in Europe.

3. Set up as a clearing house for the community, BRIC was active in the 1970s.

4. The Harriet Tubman Youth Centre, set up under the auspices of the YMCA to provide educational and recreation activities, was active in the 1970s.

5. The Jamaican Canadian Association was founded in 1962, the year Jamaica won independence from Britain. Garvey was born in Jamaica.

Cleata Morris
1924

I was born in 1924. My ancestors came to Canada ages ago
— it must have been in the very early eighteenth century.
Somewhere — now this is just a guess — in the 1830s.

They were fugitives from slavery on my father's side.
My Great-grandmother Robbins would tell us the story of
her husband: Grandpa Robbins' grandmother came up
from the South. The children's father may have been a
slave owner and he possibly sent her this way.

Their names were Calico, and travelling they happened
to see a robin, so they changed their name to Robbins. She
came here with her children and Grandma used to say she
was a beautiful lady. She was formerly from Egypt, they
tell. Grandma didn't specify if they came up through the
Underground.

The Morrises came up on the Underground Railroad. It
would seem that this is the way she possibly came, but I
can't say; I'm not sure. There were approximately five
children with her.

She settled more or less in this area, the Raleigh
Township area. The Morrises — their first settlement as far
as we know is in the Barrie area. There is a little Black

church at Oro. Looking at the plaque that they erected there, we see the names of our early ancestors. How they got to Oro, we're not sure.

Among the settlers in around there and in Collingwood, it seems to me that there was intermarriage. There was one I know that married a Scotswoman. From Oro, the Morrises in that area settled around South Buxton.

My father's grandmother on his grandfather's side — my great-grandmother — she was from Dublin, Ireland. On my mother's side, her father's grandparents were from Pennsylvania. Whether they came during the immigration of the Dutch into the New World, I don't know.

My mother's mother's parents were from the south. I know one of her great-uncles fought in the war. I'm not sure what part of the south, which makes me feel that they came afterwards. The Underground Railroad was on.

Now Great-grandma Robbins, she was always very interesting because she had so many stories about her parents and grandparents. As far as I remember about Grandma Robbins, I would consider her as a tradeswoman, but more than that a doctor, musician — you name it!

If any of us were sick, we tried to get out of Grandma's sight because we knew we had the iron and the red flannel. She'd put goose grease on your chest. She'd iron your chest, and she'd iron your chest, and you also had to take goose grease too. I remember my dad saying that when he had his tonsils out Grandma was the doctor's assistant. She put her finger in his mouth at the wrong time, so you know what happened.

Then she would sew; we never knew what it was to have clothes from the store because Grandma was always sewing for us kids. Even if you had a problem with your shoes, she was kind of a shoemaker, fixing them. She loved to sing, but Grandma couldn't cook — that's Great-grandma Robbins.

I owe lots to my mother, definitely, and to my Grandmother Morris because they always taught us that when we went out to work to always do your very best, to work out the way you would work at home, and to be very honest.

She was a good cook, she was very thrifty, and she knew how to save money. She knew what young people would do with money — we always had to give our money to her. She kept all of our money separately, and at the end of the summer period she gave us some money, and we were happy. She taught many of us the basic values; she was precious to me.

My parents were farmers. We were on a fifty-acre farm, and there wasn't always enough money to be had, so Daddy used to do a lot of ditching. He scraped the roads out on the tenth concession, Raleigh Township, and then he would also do work out for other farmers because they considered him a good horseman. The white neighbours would bring their young colts over and have Daddy train them. In his later life, he did work at Libby's canning factory. He didn't like that too well. He worked the sawmill for a while, and during his retiring years, he trained horses with Murray Drew. That's what he loved most.

My mom was more or less a housewife, although I must say that Mom worked in the fields helping Daddy with harvest crops. But he always felt that because she did so much work in the house that she wouldn't let us girls mess up her house, so he had jobs for us girls outside and kept Mom inside. Then there was a point in her life when she did market eggs, and she made butter, dressed chickens too. She'd drive the horse and buggy into Chatham, leaving at four o'clock in the morning to get her place in the market to sell her wares.

She must've done that for at least four years. One Saturday she returned home and she was quite shaken. My dad asked her what the problem was. Apparently a coloured man came back and complained to her that the chicken that she had sold to him the week before had something inside. He complained to the gentleman at the market who defended my mother — he knew that this guy was just trying to get another chicken. After that day Daddy said that there's no need for her going back to the market to take that hassle.

My mother also picked fruit on the lake for three or four years as well. The four children worked out in the fields. My dad made sure we all had chores before school. We were to carry water because we didn't have running water from the well, and each of us girls had a cow to milk first thing in the morning.

We were out at about seven-thirty in the morning because the cows were producing milk at about a quarter to eight, and it would take us about ten minutes or so. It was cold in the morning — you learn to milk fast. We did have to carry water before we went to school — carry water, carry wood. My brother had to help take care of the horses — clean out their stalls or brush the horses down. Not so much clean out the barn — that was a little heavy — put the feed in for the horses and for the cows. And then we'd have to gather eggs. After school, of course, there was milking again, carrying in wood. We still had a lot of free time; definitely our homework was always done.

In the summer, during the harvest period, we worked in the fields. And since there was only one boy, I used to get out and help my brother take the team of horses, and maybe plough, or disc, or harrow. He had a team that was driving and I had a team. I did enjoy it; I really did.

My dad, he also worked in Ann Arbor, Michigan. He had to go — we didn't have any money; so that there'd be money coming in, he would go to Ann Arbor and work during the winter. I'll never forget this — my brother, he always seemed to have so much to do; he always had so much more to do than we did. Daddy always wanted the horses exercised in the winter. We had the colts. I thought that I would try helping him exercise. I told my brother, "Look, I'll take out Queenie," — she was the calmer one; she was a little slower; she was smaller than King. "I'll take her down the road to exercise her, ok? And don't you bring King out till I get Queenie in."

So we got along very nicely, Queenie and I. My dad always said, "These aren't riding horses. You don't treat them that way." So we just walked more or less. We were on our way back — and "Neigh!" — and my brother was coming out of the barn with King that Queenie wanted to get. Naturally, she wanted to see her cousin, and she started galloping, and she pulled me. I was never a rider; I never could ride bareback, anyway. It was one side, one side, one side, and I finally fell off the horse — and Daddy said you never let a horse run away from you.

When I look back, she was dragging me and I saw her heels, so I let her go. After that I wasn't too keen; I never did share that job with my brother, but then we did have to work together.

There was another time when one of the horses was sick. We decided to doctor this horse rather than my uncle coming down to do it. We used to notice Daddy, pulling the tongue of the horse out, pulling the tongue way out, putting a loop, tying the tongue, and placing the other end of the rope over a rafter. You hold on. By that way you get the mouth wide open, and you take like one of those pop bottles — the liniment and hot warm water was in there — and you'd put it way back, that's way back — they don't have any teeth — and you'd put it way back and let it go down their throat easily.

This is what we tried. The horse had a stomachache. Afterwards my uncle came down about two hours after. The horse was doing just fine, but we were scared, very scared doing it.

There were three girls and one boy. I always felt that Hill, my brother, was doing much more than we were doing, and that's why I used to go and help him. That's why I did so much work out in the fields. Ruby and Ona, they didn't do as much as I did, but he always seemed to have quite a bit to do because we always had to keep the horses clean, brushed down and curry combed. The stalls always had to be cleaned out and that was always work. Cleaning out manure behind them, that was always his job. I didn't like it, but I done it.

My mother wouldn't allow us to clean in the house. She didn't want her kitchen messed up. We washed no dishes; we didn't get in her kitchen. And her floor — you could eat off the floor because Mom's floor was always clean. She did all of the housework. Daddy was disgusted. He would always say, "Let those girls do it," but she didn't, and he'd throw us outside.

I went to school at Raleigh. Raleigh was three-quarters white and a quarter Black. There was a Parker girl and a Chase girl. Now they were moving out and we moved in. Fern and Ona and I went.

I remember the first day: Miss Clarke, she would hold

you on her lap and I liked that! I thought everybody was
the same. As far as I was concerned, everybody was the
same. But after that — maybe it was because we were just
beginning to learn — another teacher would come in, and
you watched who they favoured, and then you felt there
was a little discrimination against someone there.

In one case we beat up a girl. She called us "nigger" or
something, so we waited till recess and whupped the
daylights out of her — and she became a teacher! There
must've been three or four on the poor girl. Taught her a
lesson, I'm sure. I don't think she even mentioned it to the
teacher because we would've likely got it from the teacher
as well, and as Daddy always said, if you get one at school
you're going to get one at home.

I went to that school up to grade eight. After we left
grade eight, I was home for a year. I got out ahead of Fern
and Ona — it was that year that we didn't have any money
to send me anywhere. My uncle in Ann Arbor wanted me
to go to school at Ann Arbor High School and I did.

I left with my grandparents in the first part of September. The immigration officer asked me, "Young lady, why
aren't you in school?" My grandpa said, "Well, we're going
to see if she can't go to school in the States." They said, "Oh
no." It was in the '30s.

I could stay only two weeks. I came home and cried,
and then they thought maybe I might like to take up
knitting. I went to a white lady and she was teaching me
how to knit — and I was contrary; I wouldn't learn how to
knit. I just had a miserable time staying at home, and then
Fern went to Merlin. We didn't have enough money still,
so Ona and I went to North Buxton.

We had no car, so we couldn't travel back and forth.
School cost money — buying books, buying clothes. We

were rather fortunate when it came to the clothes line because my grandpa used to work at sorority houses in Ann Arbor, and we always got boxes of clothes. We had the clothes, but it was transportation and buying books that we lacked. My grandfather would clean, and he would take care of the lawns, and in the winter there was the snow — he would be like the handyman around the sorority houses.

The following year Ona and I went to Buxton school — we could walk there. We took grade nine and ten with Mr. Alexander there. From there we were going to go to school in Chatham — Mom had a sister in Chatham, Aunt May and Uncle Bert. We were going to Chatham Collegiate Institute, feeling that we could stay with my aunt. We were at CCI for about one or two weeks. My aunt was a Seventh Day Adventist and she laid down the law. Also, what we weren't to eat — any meat and so forth. So my father brought us home. Then I got my driver's license and we went to Merlin.

We finished high school at Merlin. That was grade twelve and part of grade thirteen, only part because I took sick. It was during the war. The government offered any grade twelve or thirteen student who would become interested in teaching anywhere in Ontario forty-five dollars. It was a lot of money in that time — just take a six-week teacher training course. I got excited in May when this came through: I'm going to apply and I'm going to be able to make some money for the family, I thought.

Teaching was the last thing I had wanted to do because I had wanted to be a secretary, like my aunt. Norma Brown and I went to London to take this course. Both of us had our jobs before we left. Norma was in Shrewsbury. I had my school in Chatham Township. The school was on the property that my Grandpa Travis donated. He had given them the land for the school. My mother had gone to this school; it was predominantly Black. That school now was three-quarters Black and one-quarter white.

That fall, in September, I had my class. Now talk about an experience! We were fortunate that during that six-week course our teachers were inspectors. Of course, they taught us what we would normally expect in a school situation. I'm glad we did have them as teachers because otherwise I don't think I would've lasted.

The first day my dad and mother took me. I asked them to stay in front. I had a list of do-nots on foolscap — that was my bible — and then a strap beside it. I think I weighed about a hundred and five. Well, I rang the bell and those clowns came rushing in. There must've been about forty big boys — I never saw such big strapping boys — and they ran in, stood beside the desks, and I just stood. I'd be about twenty — and I just stood there and looked at them. "First," I said, "we're going to line up. Girls on one side and boys on the other side of the sidewalk. And when there is order outside, then I will tell you when you are to enter." If one of them had lunged for me, I think that would've been my end. That's how I started.

In Chatham Township I taught grades one to eight, the whole thing. It was just a one-room school. They were in rows, but I didn't have one row per grade; I'd have maybe two people over in this corner might be grade one, and maybe somebody sitting behind them were in grade three; maybe four people in grade four. They were sitting in little clusters, whatever grade, because when you started dictating spelling you'd have the speller on your arm. You'd say, "grade six" and give them their words, give grade seven their words, grade eight, and back and forth. You'd kind of have them clustered together so you wouldn't be disturbing your little groups over here who were working something out.

I did it for fourteen years. I loved it. And, in fact, after I went to Windsor to a city school, I complained to no end every year. If they had another one-room rural school, I'd be the first applicant! It wasn't any problem. The part that I disliked was you were principal and teacher; when it came to all the reports — the principal's reports — those reports were becoming so massive, that's what held you back more or less. If they'd leave you alone and let you teach — but you had to do those reports. It was the teaching that I just enjoyed.

My students did quite well in comparison with the urban students. My second year teaching, my third year teaching, I had four grade eights in for departmental examinations. Three of them were honours students and the other one did well. I think I had two failures — that's plain repeaters — in grade eight.

Then too we had music festivals. We took first prize for four-part singing. An itinerant music teacher used to come once a week, and she'd leave us a song, and we'd learn it. We had a spelling bee in Chatham Township area and one of my students took second in that. I just like to think of how they're doing now. I tell them, "Look, I don't teach you anything — it's there all the time. Just trying to get it out of you." And their eyes jump and dazzle. Even that little boy down there that's been such a little nuisance, there's something maybe he has to offer.

If they had left the rural schools as they were, I think I would still be a teacher. Then we amalgamated into an area school, Chatham Township Area School. That way we had a supervisor and principal.

Then I went to Windsor. I was an associate teacher of the faculty of the London Normal School and the University of Windsor. Then I taught at the department of education. I wasn't too keen on teaching the adults. Number one, they never do their homework — I'm shocked. That type of course was just to get another certificate to upgrade, so they can make more money; I didn't like their attitude. When it all boils down it's still back to the classroom; that's where I enjoy my work.

I much preferred the rural country. The urban school's big and impersonal in comparison. If you didn't have each child in your class at heart, they could become lost in this school. Just lost and totally forgotten. Then there's that in the urban where the children expect you to do something for them; they expect you to do more. Sometimes you would get the parents too — you'd have a different cross-section. You would have a different type of parent there too — all professions, all types — and in the rural schools, you'd just have the farmers, and that would make a difference.

One year, the principal came in and said, "Is your report ready?" I said, "It will be ready, ok?" and I stalled for time, really stalled. He came back, and he said, "Look, is it ready?" I said I was working on it. And he said, "I've got to go to a meeting and these things have got to be in." So he started through and he put a checkmark beside the Black names. The principal put an X beside all Blacks. And I've filled these things out for umpteen years! What could it mean when they put it like that, except they're starting to label these kids.

They wanted to keep track of every student in Windsor, and what he or she was capable of doing, and who they were going to shove into the remedial classes.

Looking over the situation, you can see that most of them are ours, which really annoys me. I would go to the parents, and I would say, "Get behind those teachers. Raise more fuss. Go to school boards. Make yourselves heard. This is what is happening — don't let them put your kids there." Some of them would do something about it.

I initiated some sort of campaign among the parents of these students. I was able to talk with parents when we had parent-teacher interviews. I would call parents in. I can remember on one occasion they had a feeling that Morris is down there talking, and the principal would kind of duck in for something. I was just waiting till he left.

I would often call the parents in when I thought that there was something. Even some of the poor white children, they were discriminated against as well. As far as I am concerned, it is still a major problem, and I don't think that it's going to get any better. It will if we have Black teachers who will stand up — and I mean stand!

I tried to prevent them from entering the special classes. But they knew how we would work, and they might wait until the kid got into another grade, and then they'd start working on that child, but they wouldn't try it in our class. They'd even come and ask us what did the child know. But the next thing you knew the child was in a special class and you wondered why. Now in many cases they were trying to convince the parents that they would be there for a short while, and then they would move back into the regular class. This is what they did when they saw that the parent may be questioning it. They would say "Just for a while," but very often they didn't get back into the mainstream.

Part of the problem could've been the teachers — that they had subsequently were not as supportive of them — so the child maybe became more reserved. We have too many misfits in the teaching profession, too many people who end up in teaching because they can't do anything else. They're there to say that they're teachers and they're there because they feel that they're secure. They're going to put in their time — but not for the child at heart, just what they are getting out of it.

I've worked hours after hours and at home on the weekends. You'd work in committees for the City of Windsor, then you'd do a lot of your work at home, and then you'd go on meetings every week. I was the only Black teacher on those committees — all volunteer. I was asked, so I couldn't say no.

Before I went to Windsor — around Buxton — I was involved in teaching Sunday school and in church work and missionary work. The reason I didn't get married was when I was going to school we were always so poor: we didn't have lights; we didn't have anything. We didn't have electricity; we had no car. Grandpa Shadd used to pile us all in the rumble seat of the car and we'd go into Chatham and get ice-cream cones. Mom, even when she was younger, she had a murmuring heart. Daddy and all his work — he had duodenal ulcers. When I started teaching I thought of my parents: they've seen that we've had food; we've had love, all of this; let's try to make life a little easier. So I shunned these other things — I'm not interested; I've got to make money. I've got to take care of my parents — that was my aim. I've got to make them comfortable. Of course, if there was anything left later for me, then maybe — but then too I just didn't seem to be too interested at that time. I was more interested in my career and enjoying what I was doing and wanting to help my parents.

Then in Windsor I got involved in the Hour A Day

Study Club. When the club was founded we studied Black history an hour a day — it was our duty. I've been a member for at least twenty-five years. We have a scholarship fund. It used to be the Mother's Club in the 1930s, connected to the local council of Women of Windsor since back then.

I think I've been discriminated more as a Black person than as a woman, really. I think it's been as a person because when we go to places, even to eat, it was not because I'm a woman but because I was a Black person.

It seems to me that the maternal role has been so strong that Black women seem to be mothers to everybody, even to the whites in some cases. Just thinking of some, there seems to be a more natural or motherly role. And the white women, in some cases it seems as if they're there for the convenience of their husbands!

I always upgraded my educational background. I was always back in school at University of Windsor. I got my B.A; my major was history. I thought it would be good to do something on Buxton, like a sociological history. I told the professor what I wanted and he said if he didn't like it I'd get a D. And I said, "I know." It didn't upset me in the least.

Fern Shadd Shreve
1924

I was born in 1924. My grandparents were born in Canada, as well as my parents. All my life — as far back as I can remember — our family lived in a rural setting.

The original Shadds came in the 1830s and they came from Pennsylvania. They weren't fugitives, they weren't slaves: they were free Blacks. Shadd was an abolitionist. He wasn't happy with the educational system in the United States. He brought his children to Canada to be educated, and he became very active in the abolitionist movement here in Canada. He was the father of thirteen children.

From the Abraham Shadd[1] family came this outstanding person, Mary Ann.[2] She was a school teacher, a newspaper editor. There's a story that comes to my mind right now. I have some letters, some copies of some letters that her sister had written to other members of the family — this was Elizabeth, the missionary. She said that in some way sister Mary Ann would be better off remaining at home with her children. She obviously didn't approve of Mary Ann and the way Mary Ann travelled around the country. She was raising money, basically, I think, to try and keep that newspaper going.[3]

She was a speaker, a public speaker, and as a woman in those days that was really something outstanding too. Eventually, she became a lawyer at the age of sixty, and when the book was written about her I read it, and I could identify through her. I could see myself being her — the fact that she was outspoken and honest and demanded high standards from other people. I feel I have those characteristics, and I could certainly identify with everything she said.

One of the things that she pushed against was Blacks segregating themselves from the white churches — she admonished them not to do that. I keep thinking if she could see today the Black churches and the condition that they're in that she'd say, "I told you so."

I think maybe if you're involved in the Black churches you would almost know what I'm saying. The attendance is down drastically, and they are not functioning as I feel the way a church functions to each programme and that sort of thing. They're not progressing, and the younger people are not following through into the Black churches, and I know for sure that in the bigger cities the people attend neighbourhood churches. Regardless of who you are or where you are, you go to the church in your neighbourhood. That's the way it should be.

My grandmothers, they were both farm wives. We lived across the road from Grandpa and Grandma Shadd. I remember them as authority figures — the same as our father and mother, only the extended family, I suppose you could say. I remember Grandma Shadd as being a very austere person; she was very frugal and we sort of looked on her with respect. She didn't demonstrate a feeling of warmth. Grandpa Shadd laughed a lot, and we felt that was okay, but he could be also very stern.

Our Prince grandparents, on the other side of the family, lived on the eighth concession in Raleigh, which was a couple of miles north of us, so we didn't see them as often, but we had great fondness for them. Grandma Prince was very, very generous with her clothing and money, and we used to enjoy spending two weeks' vacation there because she would take us to Chatham to shop, and that was something that we, in our youth, were not privileged to do. We longed to get to Grandma Prince's 'cause that was the highlight of our life at that point. She said that we were welcome to come until we started to date and then she wasn't going to accept the responsibility for us as teenagers who were dating. That's kind of funny now! There must've been some Indian blood in Grandma Prince's family because of the facial features. She had very straight hair and high cheekbones, that sort of thing.

Grandma Shadd was an orphan and she was left on the doorstep of the Doo family. In the registry office I got a copy of the original land ownership, and I assume that is part of the Elgin settlement land.[4] One of the Doos had fifty acres of this land. Eventually it belonged to a Julia Doo, who, I believe, was her mother, and eventually down the road it became property of Mary and Flavius Shadd — Mary was Mary Doo.

Grandma Shadd was a housewife and did the duties of a good housewife: keeping the house tidy and preparing the meals and serving them, cleaning up after. I don't recall that either of my grandmothers worked in the fields or did anything outside of the home; certainly there was no jobs or employment outside of the home.

She was very frugal 'cause they had had perhaps a tough time in life. She managed the money — seemed to dole out the money — and was very, very careful as to how she did this. Grandma had that characteristic all her life, so that being poor somewhere along the line must've created it in her to be very, very careful as to how she spent the money.

Being raised on the farm was the one thing that made my life comfortable at that time. In the Depression I do not recall ever being hungry. It must've been a very comfortable time in my life because I don't have memories of it. The only thing that I do recall my mother saying — this would be some years later — that she thought she could never look another bean in the face! Beans being a staple food that you could grow on the farm, we must've been eating a lot of beans.

We worked hard on the farms; there were six of us and we each — four sisters and two brothers — we hoed and we blocked beets. You drill the beets in with seed: they're too thick; they have to be separated so that they can expand and grow. You have to chop out spaces between the seed, so that there is about a foot between each plant. That was something you had to do. You did that in the early spring. In the fall you topped them: you had a hook knife to pull the beet out of the ground and chop the top off, throw them in the pile, load the piles in the truck and take them to the factory.

In the spring we planted tomatoes. We did planting; we did everything. The good memories I'm sure I've forgotten, but these memories you never forget. We hated that work so much, but we were required to do it. And I often wonder sometimes how we got our education because we were out in May, June — off and on — doing these beets, planting these tomatoes. We took off school to do it. How I ever completed my high school education, I'll never know. I must've worked hard to do that too. Today I can appreciate the fact that we were taught that hard work is wholesome because I respect hard work, and I look today sometimes and I think how lightly people get off from doing hard work. There really isn't much hard work anymore. Mental work can be hard — I understand that too — but this physical labour that we did on that farm, it was something else.

I felt sorry for my mother because she, in a good many cases, worked right along with us in the field, but in addition to that, she also had the housework that had to be done. We kids helped at that time. But it wasn't easy. A lot of things that you know went on, sometimes you wonder about. But I'm sure that my mother's life was not an easy one, as far as being a farmer's wife.

My mother was a very tender-hearted, loving person. She didn't demonstrate it particularly, but you just felt it when you were around her. She was industrious, of course. She had chickens and pigs — the pigs would be in the part of the barn which was the man's building, really. There's a story of how she used to kill a chicken. She would grab a chicken by its head and whip it around — and then grab the body with the other hand — and she could pull those heads off those chickens just like you've never seen. The chicken would go one way and the head would go another way. They used to flop around on the ground till they were totally dead. The thing that sticks in my mind is how she could do that — for me this was out of character for her. With her tender heart and her loving disposition, she could really whip those heads off those chickens!

One time this fellow used to travel around the country buying cattle. He was a Jewish fellow, and he had come for to buy some cattle, and he would also buy some eggs if we had any there. I think she had maybe nine eggs or six eggs in the house, and she sent me out to pick the eggs out of the nest that were out there. Instead of getting three, like I was supposed to, I decided to get some more. In the end, in trying to get these eggs, I dropped and broke all of them! I got a real chastisement over that job! The eggs would be laid in. We had an old shed and it would be made of planks. Then it would be covered with straw from the wheat harvest. The hens would lay their eggs in the straw, so you had to search around and find the hollow spot where these eggs would be laid. That's what I was doing, looking for a nest, when I spilt the whole bunch.

The crops that were easy were wheat and corn. Today, soy beans is a big crop, but I can't recall soy beans. When it came to wheat harvest you only had to set up the shucks and with the corn you had to set up the shucks, tear them down. The binder cuts the grain and spit it out in what we call shocks, and so we'd have to go behind the binder and pick up the shocks and pile them together to make a stook.

When they would thresh that grain they'd go down the field with the horse and wagon and pitch those stooks on the wagons and take them up to the threshing machine. With corn it was similar: we usually took the stalks apart, tore them open and husked the corn — took the ears off the stalks. We used to put them in piles. They'd come along again with wagons, bushel baskets, load that up and put it into the wagons. I tell you there was nothing easy about farming.

The only thing I used to say was the boys got all the easy work. They drove the tractors when the tractors came, and we'd be labouring away back there, doing all this other hard work, and they'd be driving the tractor.

We used to go round from field to field, hoeing or doing beets or whatever had to be done. By this time we had learned to drive the car a little bit. Thomas, my brother, would drive or I would drive. He and I got in a big fight this day over who would drive. I guess I won the battle. I drove home and drove right into the wall of the garage!

There were certain cattle that would be for sale — beef cattle — and then, of course, we had milk or dairy cattle, and it was our responsibility to milk those cows twice a day. We milked before we went to school and in the evening, before supper. Each of us had our own cow and we'd be responsible for seeing that that cow got milked. We had a separator and we separated the milk from the cream. It was a busy life, really. In all my teen years I was working on the farm. When I went away to London to go to school that would be about the end of my farm past.

I went through elementary school and stopped at about grade eight and took a year off because I didn't want to go to school. They taught grade nine and ten level here at the Buxton school. I decided I didn't want to do that — or somebody decided. I don't know whether I made the decision or my dad! After a year at home — it was the most lonely time because all the rest of the kids were in school — I went back to school and then district high school that next year. I never really left school for the rest of my life till I retired!

I started high school out in Merlin. The grade thirteens were so small in number. I can remember being in grade nine and grade thirteen class; we were at the back of our room. After grade ten, the school burned down during the summer and we went back that fall. The remainder of my days were spent in old dilapidated buildings in the village, trying to get an education the best way that you could. It was really, really rough. The men teachers had gone away to war at that point and so we had all women. There were only three or four teachers at the most. We had one toilet for all the kids in the building — it was an old hotel, with apartments above — little kids running, radios playing. We had a rough time in our last three years of high school, but we stuck it out.

Back in the elementary days, we were again in the minority — there were only two families in the school, a predominantly white school — and we just enjoyed each other. There was never really any problems. When we went to high school the same thing really. There might be the odd name calling, and you talked to the other guy and went on about your business — that's the only thing. Basically, there really wasn't, as far as I'm concerned, any difference shown as to whether you were Black or white. There wasn't that many of us to start with.

I think that my teaching just sort of evolved in that when you decided to take high school you were expected to do something with it. There were not that many opportunities other than London Normal School.

The normal school was what a girl could go into at that time. Because education was part of our family tradition, it just seems to me now that it must've been a part of the plan, that I just drifted into it. I've been told that my father was advised that I should get an education.

Marion Griffiths was the one who told me this story. She said that because I had showed promise that my father should see that I get an education. And Marion said that was because of Aunt Mabel, who had a mental breakdown at the age of nineteen. I was told that the reason for it was the fact that she had wanted an education and was denied this, due to the fact that there was not enough money available to send her to school. Unfortunately, Aunt Mabel has been in this institution since the age of nineteen until the present day.

She's still alive. She was born in 1898. She's two years older than my dad. I don't really know the full story because my family never talked about her very much. I didn't know anything about it when I was growing up. It wasn't until I got old enough to be aware that every time there was a death in the family, her name was on the obituary list. I would say to my dad, "Who is this Mabel?" He just refused to talk about it. In those days it was a mark on the family if there was mental illness in the family. It wasn't until after he died in '73 — and Aunt Julia a few years later — we tracked her down and discovered where she was and we went to visit her. They said that she was very intelligent and was determined to have an education and wasn't allowed.

The day the war ended the whole city of London closed down. We had the first sit-in — we felt that if they could close down, why should we be in class? There was a wide sweeping stairway, and we all sat down on the stairway. But the principal came, and after he gave a lecture of how we were being trained to teach the next generation and how we should go back to our classrooms, we very obediently went back to our classrooms.

In '44, '45 I graduated — same year the war ended. There weren't a lot of choices for women as far as working outside of the home. Mostly women attended the normal school. I was the only Black in the school. There were about six men. We had a hundred and some odd. One of the reasons that there was not men was because the war was on. London Normal School — believe me there was nothing normal about it! I don't know where they picked up that name. The previous name was the model school. So the older teachers went to a model school; I went to a normal school, which was a teachers' college.

I'm a person that gets along well with people most of the time, and I think that at that stage of the game I had gone to school with whites all my life, so it was just kind of a way of life. I didn't feel very different, really. Now that I sit and I look back on it, I realize that I really didn't participate too freely in the social aspect. I had no partner to go to the dances with and things of that nature, so I didn't go. If things were held during daytime, during classtime, I was always involved in that, but I was not really a part of the social life of the school.

When I finished teachers' college I taught in my home school. The reason that I was able to get that job was because my father was a member of the school board. After having been there a year my son was born — I married and my son was born. Then I tried to go back, and I wasn't accepted back because, in the meantime, Dad had bought the property and moved to Buxton. He was no longer a member of that board. For seven years I was without a job because there was no Black school. That was really my first experience that sticks out in my mind of discrimination: Black teachers were not allowed to teach in the white schools.

There was an ad in the Chatham paper and they wanted teachers. So Verlyn Ladd and I were teaching over here. We decided just for the heck of it to submit an application. Nothing, of course, happened, and about a month later, they ran their ad again and I got angry. I called the director of education. "How can you be advertising for teachers? And I know two applications you didn't even acknowledge." "Oh. What are your qualifications?" And I gave them and he called me back. Their policy was they didn't hire married women; they didn't hire teachers over a certain age.

I do know that that same year Verlyn applied to Windsor and got a job, so it was opening up — about '64. The reason I know that date is that I taught public school — the kindergarten-junior room — over here for four years in the North Buxton School. When Verlyn went to Windsor I moved into the senior level. There was another girl who had applied to the Chatham school; she had come up through the system. Her name was Jackson. His excuse to her was he was hiring alphabetically and stopped at H!

I stopped teaching for seven years and I raised my son until 1955. Then I started teaching again. I retired in 1980. In '68–'69, they closed this school, this section number 13, and Raleigh became a consolidated school at Merlin, so the kids were bussed to that school.[5] You can look at it two ways: for the children, they got to know so many other children from various areas of the township, and that had its good and bad effects because it used to be that when we were in a small rural school we did not have to do yard duty, for the children policed themselves, their peers.

For children there were opportunities because of the materials which you could offer in a consolidated situation. But it pretty near destroyed the Buxton community because there was no focus — the school was the core of the community, and the school kept the community together, a family type of thing. The kids go from Merlin to high school; some go to Blenheim, some go to Tilbury. There are two or three different ones in Chatham, so they have lost their ties in a sense with the community.

The community hasn't been the same since. The closeness of the kids because they become friends with the classmates, their peers. They don't even know each other as well as maybe they should anymore.

Teaching in North Buxton School, I started out in the

junior level, grades one to four. Four years later, when the senior teacher Verlyn Ladd left, then I became the senior teacher, also classified as the principal, which I didn't really know meant much in those days. The day we left — the final day of the tenancy of the school was at Christmas time — we'd had a Christmas party. We were all wrapping up everything to leave; we'd boxed everything, and Trudy Shadd wrapped her arms around me, and we cried some tears and said "Oh, it'll never be the same."

Many times people will say things that I don't even remember, events that took place at the school that are positive. I think of the kids who are now men and women who live in this community: some of them still call me Mrs. Shreve; they just can't drop that Mrs. ... Yet it was funny. One girl, who shall remain nameless — she wasn't a bad kid, but she was a nuisance and not a very good attendant — she couldn't wait till the door closed to call me Fern. It was so funny.

I had a little girl call me the other day and wish me a happy birthday 'cause I had taught her — this was in Merlin now — and she saw my name on the calendar. And that same Trudy Shadd sent me a birthday card this year.

I started out as a wife and I guess I've always been ambitious. We had to have money and that wasn't easy to come by. I used to work in the store — that was before there was a school. My parents had a general store. Gene, my husband, owned a truck and the truck was very expensive to keep up — the license — and the work was not there. He enjoyed that sort of thing — he was self-employed, like he owned these trucks. He had two at one time; the biggest problem was there wasn't enough work to make money.

The first part of my life was such a struggle to get money, to have enough money to survive on. If it hadn't been for the Shadd store, we would've had problems. We tried to raise some pigs and chickens to see if that would be profitable.

I got married in 1946. I remember working at seasonal work at Libby's, where you'd work on the tomato lines. Tomatoes again. In Libby's factory, you stood beside a moving line and picked off the bad tomatoes. One other thing that I did was to unload the baskets of juice cans — and they were the big juice cans, forty-eight ounces. I had to put those from the baskets on to the conveyer as it passed, and the thing that bugged me — it is back-breaking work — this man was sitting about three feet from me with a stick in his hand, watching the cans go around, making sure that they're straight on the conveyor belt. Honestly, the more I think about that, the angrier I get. He got that easy job over the one I had — I don't know!

The thing in my mind is that we were constantly concerned about how we were going to have enough money to survive. I struggled working part-time and that sort of thing. My mother was very helpful. She helped with all my children, my sisters' too — even raised the second generation until we realized that she doesn't need to do that anymore. We took my mother so much for granted; we assumed that she was going to be there to look after the kids.

Going back to the marriage thing, with my husband I always wanted to be a part of community things, and he more or less told me that I couldn't go. And I remember him going to sleep and I sneaked out of the house. Can you imagine doing something like that today?! It just wouldn't be because I wouldn't allow it! I just don't know how eventually he accepted the fact that I was going. We never really talked about it; our communication was not always the best. We kind of communicated just on understanding things: I'm supposed to know what you're thinking.

Everybody was in the same boat. What your problem is everybody else is doing or trying to do. The factory work was full of people like myself trying to make a buck. There were men there too. There were other women like myself there, doing the same thing.

Another place we worked during the winter. Gene had bought this red truck and he drove us to work in this great big red truck. There was Ivy Brown and Gwen Robbins. He would drive us into work and pick us up. We were working with British Leaf Tobacco Factory and then we worked stemming. We took a leaf and then somehow or other we removed the stem from the leaf. That was a job that you worked hard. You sat down, or you stood up, whichever you pleased, but you were paid by the pound, so you had to work like heck to make any kind of money 'cause tobacco is light.

When I came back from London in 1945 I went to work in a munitions plant, working with hand grenades. We were preparing these shells — we didn't have anything to do with the explosives — they were dipped and scrapped and stuff like that. We weren't making much money there — they didn't pay money in those days, but you could get work like it was going out of style. It was night work — we worked nights all the time in the munitions plant. I decided that wasn't quite enough money for me, so I'd go out on Saturday and work extra. I went to the unemployment office and they sent me to this lady's house to wash. When I get there she wants me to wash her bathroom, and as slow as I worked I think I made two dollars — and it was something like fifty cents an hour I was being paid. I didn't go to work any more Saturdays!

I remember in the munitions factory — Chatco Steel in Chatham — that was where there were more Blacks than any other job that I think that I worked on. I don't know why, but there were whites there. I guess if I wanted to make a case of it, I could probably say that the Blacks were doing the dirtier work, but I can't prove that. There was a lady, an older lady, Mrs. Selby, and they had what they called the oven. These things were dipped in varnish, and then they were cooked, and they'd go around, and poor Mrs. Selby would sit under there and take those things off. Today, I would just think that would be the most horrible thing that I could think of. We were also so much younger than she — we should've been doing some of that dirty work. That was really terrible. We worked nights. She'd be sitting there, nodding, see the fire burning, and go "Oh!" I think back on it now and think that's just dreadful! Why was she chosen to do that particular job?

There were no Blacks working in stores. I remember vividly visiting Janie Anderson, who was operating an elevator in Eaton's store, and another lady too. They worked shifts — operated the elevator.

I've done a lot of things when I used to think back. When I finished high school, before starting school in the fall, I went to work at the public general hospital, cleaning floors. I was there for a really short time.

I used to walk. I lived with Aunt Julia on Wellington Street East, and then I walked from the hospital there, back and forth. There was a hub grill. I used to stop in there for a talk or something. I remember Gene and I went in there one night, like after work, and they wouldn't serve us, and to this day I do not know why. They served me as a single person, but they wouldn't serve us as a couple.

Gene used to go with his trucking friends to drink beer

at Montreal House in Chatham. He enjoyed that. When they finished work on Saturdays that's where they would hang out. So his sister, Betty, and her husband were coming up from Detroit. We wanted to go out some place socially. So he took them to the Montreal House, and they wouldn't serve us. We were married, and so were Paul and Betty, so it would be in the '50s, at least. Somebody will come and say, "I'm sorry. I can't serve you." And you look at them with your mouth open and you eventually walk out!

There were people in Chatham — Elvin Ladd it was — who had an organization, similar to what Phillip Shadd worked with. Community League it was called. They took that case up because they had experienced the same thing with the Montreal House. What the outcome was I can't tell you because I don't remember. Certainly in the '50s it was still happening and in the schools up to the '60s.

Merlin had a bad reputation. The funniest thing is that I don't have any bad memories about it. In high school one of my best friends was a white girl. We didn't have boyfriends with cars, and she would come up all way down to our house and take us to the dances and things like that. I guess I have a tendency only to remember the good times!

I've been a member of the Community Club it seems like for a lifetime. The things that have been done by the Community Club for the good of the village are honourable things. I have a great pride in feeling that I'm a part of that. The extension of the Community Club — the museum which was opened in 1967 — this is a project that certainly grows on you.

Arlie Robbins introduced me to an interest in the museum, which held the history of this community. It gets to be a real point of interest in my life and certainly a sense of pride in the fact that we as the Black community have contributed to the history of southwestern Ontario. I think for me that's my greatest part. Now I volunteer my time for the museum: sometimes as curator, guide — whatever is to be done that I can do physically, I enjoy doing.

My son went on to teaching too. I think he is part of the chain of Shadd history, where it was his turn to be a teacher in that chain. That's what I was talking about the kids. I just wonder which one of his three kids will be that chain.

I look at myself as me, not as a woman, or as a Black, and I want people to take me as they find me, and not as a Black, or as a woman, or as a woman who is Black. It's just that I hope that it's just the me that shows through, and you like me for me, not because I'm Black or a woman.

Notes

1. Abraham Shadd, abolitionist, sat on the Raleigh Town Council in 1859. See Winks, *op. cit.*, p. 215.

2. For more information on the life and work of Mary Ann Shadd, see Winks.

3. Mary Ann Shadd ran *The Provincial Freeman* in the 1850s. She was the first woman to edit a newspaper in Canada.

4. Elgin Settlement established by William King, a Presbyterian, in 1849, was to be a model Black settlement. See Winks pp. 208–216.

5. The consolidation of schools ended *de facto* desegregation for Black schools in Ontario.

Bibliography

Braithwaite, Rella. *The Black Woman in Canada*. Toronto, self-published, 1976.

Giddings, Paula. *When And Where I Enter: The Impact of Black Women on Race and Sex in America*. New York, Bantam Books, 1985.

Hill, Daniel G. *The Freedom Seekers: Blacks in Early Canada*. Agincourt, The Book Society of Canada Ltd., 1981.

Jacques-Garvey, Amy. *Philosophy and Opinions of Marcus Garvey*. New York, Atheneum, 1923.

Jones, Jacqueline. *Labour of Love, Labour of Sorrow: Black Women, Work and the Family, From Slavery to the Present*. New York, Vintage Books, Random House, 1985.

Kelly, Joan. *Women, History and Theory*. London, University of Chicago Press, 1984.

Lerner, Gerda, ed. *Black Women in White America: A Documentary History*. New York, Vintage Books, 1973.

Leslie, Genevieve."Domestic Service in Canada, 1880–20." In Janice Acton, Penny Goldsmith and Bonnie Sheppard, eds. *Women at Work: Ontario 1850–1930*. Toronto, Women's Press, 1974.

Magill, Dennis William. *Africville: The Life and Death of a Canadian Black Community*. Toronto, McClelland and Stewart, 1974.

Martin, Linda and Kerry Segrave. *The Servant Problem*. North Carolina and London, McFarland & Company, 1985.

Painter, Nell Irvin. *The Narrative of Hosea Hudson: His Life as a Negro Communist in the South*. Cambridge and London, Harvard University Press, 1979.

Pierson, Ruth Roach. *"They're Still Woman After All": The*

Second World War and Canadian Womanhood. Toronto, McClelland and Stewart Limited, 1986.

Prentice, Alison. et al. *Canadian Women: A History.* Toronto, Harcourt Brace Jovanovich, 1988.

Ripley, C. Peter, ed. *The Abolitionist Papers*, vol. II. Chapel Hill and London, The University of North Carolina Press, 1986.

Robbins, Arlie. *Legacy to Buxton.* Self-published.

Spivak, Gayatri. "Three Women's Texts and a Critique of Imperialism." In Henry Louis Gates Jr., ed., *Race, Writing and Difference.* Chicago and London, The University of Chicago Press, 1986.

Sterling, Dorothy. *We Are Your Sisters.* New York, W.W. Norton and Company, 1984.

Tulloch, H. *Black Canadians: A Long Line of Fighters.* Toronto, NC Press, 1975.

Walker, James St. G. *A History of Blacks in Canada: A Study Guide.* Ottawa, Ministry of State-Multiculturalism, 1981.

White, Deborah Gray. *Ar'n't I a Woman? Female Slaves in the Plantation South.* New York, W.W. Norton and Company, 1985.

Winks, Robin W. *The Blacks in Canada: A History.* Montreal, New Haven and London, McGill-Queen's University Press and Yale University Press, 1971.

Photo by Lois Siegel

DIONNE BRAND is a Black poet and writer living in Toronto. She has published six books of poetry. Her latest, *No Language Is Neutral*, was nominated for a Governor General's Award in 1990.

She has also published a book of short stories, *Sans Souci and Other Stories*, and co-authored a work of non-fiction, *Rivers Have Sources Trees Have Roots — Speaking of Racism*.

Brand also works in documentary film. She was the associate director and writer of *Older, Stronger, Wiser*, a portrait film about older Black women in Canada, and she was the co-director of *Sisters in the Struggle*, a documentary about contemporary Black women activists in Canada. She is currently working on a third film *Batari Wimmin's Blues*.

Brand was Writer in Residence at the University of Toronto in 1990–91 and is now an assistant professor in the English department at University of Guelph.